Nero and the Art of Tyranny

HARETH AL BUSTANI

First published in 2021 by Sharpe Books.

*This book is dedicated to Joanne, Raffi & Yoshi,
for giving more love, support and generosity
than any one person deserves.*

CONTENTS

Prologue

The plot was hatched. Emperor Nero had to go. It didn't matter that he and his mother had already killed off the rest of the royal bloodline. Even if it meant chaos, he simply had to go.

Years ago, he promised his reign would be different, that it would be free of the arbitrary tyranny that so plagued the courts of his predecessors. And, to his credit, for a while it was. Advised by Rome's greatest philosopher, and its greatest general, Nero had started out so promising, restoring dignity to the Senate, and wiping out corruption from his court.

Those first five years of his rule would later be celebrated as the greatest of all time. In that period, he built wonderous works, scored remarkable military victories abroad and earned the love of senators, soldiers, nobles and commoners alike. He dreamed of liberating the masses from taxation and delivered greater spectacles than any that had ever come before. In generosity, he was gracious, and in discipline, fair. Most remarkably, he achieved all of this while fighting off the predatory machinations of his power-obsessed mother.

But by the summer of 64, something had changed. The emperor had turned. He was losing his mind. There had been omens, but none had been heeded. Under his watch, the great capital itself had burned to the ground. Although Nero blamed it on an obscure Jewish sect, who he tortured with rapacious delight, many held him personally responsible. Worst of all, he had incurred the wrath of the gods by singing on stage like a common Greek street urchin.

The crimes he now stood accused of were unforgivable. They transcended the sins of any of his Julio-Claudian predecessors; as megalomaniacal, tyrannical, and demented as they were. The first emperor, Augustus, would be rolling in his grave to know how low his successors had sunk. His wretched family had amassed more power than any man in Rome's history, only to be driven mad by it. How many men and women had been killed to line their paths to the throne? How many more must perish?

Nero's entire life had been a race to the top. And yet, even though he had won the greatest race of all, he still debased himself to play charioteer in full view of the commoners. Well, if he loved the races so much, let him go to the races. That's where they'd do it. They'd seize his feet, surround him, and stab him to death, just like the power-hungry Julius Caesar, and that maniac Caligula after him. Let it be a lesson for generations to come, what happens to tyrants who abuse the trust placed in them by the Roman people.

For crimes against the very honour of Rome, Nero must die.

Chapter 1: The Winds of Fortune

As winter drew 15AD to a chilly close, Rome was just beginning to adjust to life without its first emperor. The adopted son of Julius Caesar, Augustus had not only ended a century of civil war with his 31BC victory over Mark Antony, but in the ensuing decades, transformed the republic into an empire, with the conquests of Egypt, northern Spain, and central Europe. All the while, feigning reluctance, he quietly amassed an unprecedented level of power, achieving what even the mighty Caesar could not; becoming dictator for life. Without being shanked to death.

Despite his stratospheric rise to power, when it came to succession-planning, Augustus was cursed. Having produced no sons, when his two grandsons died suddenly, he was forced to turn to his dour stepson Tiberius. Tiberius had made a name for himself over a long and storied military career, carving out huge swathes of territory for Rome along the River Danube. However, the grizzled veteran was to be little more than a placeholder for Augustus's Julio-Claudian bloodline, and everyone knew it. As admired as Tiberius was, he lacked the charm that Augustus had wielded to such dramatic effect, convincing the Senate it was their idea to hand him ultimate authority, piece by piece.

When the emperor finally adopted Tiberius as his heir, it was on the condition that he would in turn adopt

Germanicus, the grandson of Augustus's sister Octavia and Mark Antony. With no precedent in place, Augustus believed that the simplest way to establish an enduring system for peaceful transitions of power was through his bloodline. Tiberius had enough clout to sit on the throne, but only to keep it warm for the children of Germanicus.

To legitimise his claim, Tiberius was forced to divorce his beloved wife and marry Augustus's notoriously promiscuous daughter, Julia. Though he wore a stern face, it masked a heavy heart. On one occasion, when he caught a passing glimpse of his ex-wife, he wept with such anguish, his courtiers made sure they never crossed paths again. His tears were churned into bitter rage by Julia's repeating cuckolding, which grew so outlandish Augustus was compelled to banish her from Rome.

But that was all in the past now. Augustus had died and been declared a god, leaving gloomy Tiberius behind to fill the exhausted treasury, and a seriously colossal pair of shoes. As the new emperor navigated the perilous straits of imperial administration and Roman society, his adopted son Germanicus continued to chase glory along the Rhine. Years earlier, Rome had suffered a devastating loss of three legions and standards to a confederation of Germanic tribes in Teutoburg Forest. Though Augustus claimed to have established the empire's natural boundaries, Germanicus was compelled to avenge the humiliation suffered in Germania. It was there, in the outpost of Oppidum Ubiorum, that his wife Agrippina gave birth to their first daughter, whom the matriarch naturally named after herself.

Agrippina the Younger's entry into the world was an auspicious one; born with two canine teeth on her upper right jaw, she was quite clearly blessed by the gods. It was an omen befitting her father, whose exploits along the Rhine would soon turn him into a living legend. After putting down a revolt by paying his men out of his own pocket, he went on to reclaim two of the three legionary eagles lost at Teutoburg, massacring scores of Germanic tribesmen along the way.

Having restored Rome's dignity, Germanicus returned home a genuine hero, enjoying the first full military triumph parade since Augustus's own in 29BC. The man of the hour was joined aboard his triumphal chariot by his five children, trailed by an endless caravan of plunder and captives, with reconstructions of his adventures abroad, enveloped by the red-hot roars of an ecstatic entourage of Roman revellers. With many comparing the young prodigy to Alexander the Great, his reputation erupted into mythical status. Unlike Tiberius, he was not just admired. He was loved; by the Senate, legions and commoners alike. His son, Gaius, had so amused the German legions waddling around in his little soldier's uniform, they started calling him 'Caligula', or 'Little Boot'. Or, more accurately, 'Bootikins'.

Tiberius later had Germanicus sent East, to set up a puppet king in the leaderless Armenia, a buffer kingdom between Rome and the Persian empire of Parthia. He would never return. In the autumn of 19AD, while travelling to Syria, Germanicus fell ill and died, just 33-years-old. Although Syria was riddled with disease and pestilence, the dying Germanicus swore that the local governor had poisoned him. His afflicted body was displayed in Antioch, as proof of his murder, before being cremated in a public funeral.

Joined by her son 'Caligula', Agrippina the Elder's long journey home from Syria was accompanied by throngs of mourning Romans, lamenting the loss of their great hero. Returning to Rome, as she laid her husband to rest in the solemn mausoleum of Augustus, Agrippina was hailed "the glory of her country, the last of Augustus's line, an unmatched example of ancient virtues". Tiberius's absence from the ceremony fuelled rumours that he had ordered Germanicus' death in a fit of paranoid envy. When the subsequent murder investigation resulted in the accused governor's suicide, many speculated the emperor had killed him off to keep a lid on his own complicity.

While her family reeled in despair, the widowed Agrippina the Elder readied her resolve against the fickle winds of fortune. Having seen her own mother sent into exile, she knew well that the thread that bound her children to the throne was a fine tightrope, stretched precariously between riches and ruin. To her relief, Tiberius placed her children under the protection of his only biological son, Drusus, and even thrust the eldest into the political limelight. Under Drusus' wing, the children were shielded from the pervasive reach of his increasingly powerful rival, Lucius Strabo Sejanus.

As Praetorian Prefect, Sejanus led the Praetorian Guard, a special military force of 10,000 men established by Augustus to serve as his personal bodyguard. As the only soldiers allowed to maintain a military presence in Rome, they wielded considerable power. Although the Guard technically answered to the emperor alone, Sejanus transformed his position into a vehicle for his own political ambitions. Hostilities soon boiled over, when Sejanus supposedly seduced Drusus' wife, and poisoned the hapless Drusus himself, leaving Germanicus' two eldest sons the only candidates left for succession.

The catastrophic loss of his only biological son was too much for Tiberius to bear. Withdrawing from public life, the distraught emperor retreated to the island of Capri. Becoming increasingly oblivious to the state of the empire, he essentially handed Sejanus free reign, which the schemer happily abused. Desperate to rid himself of rivals, Sejanus had Agrippina the Elder exiled alongside her eldest son, and her second son locked up in Rome.

When Tiberius finally realised how much his complacency had threatened the Julio-Claudian dynasty, he summoned the young Caligula to Capri, to protect him. Meanwhile, the 13-year-old Agrippina the Younger was married off to Gnaeus Domitus Ahenobarbus, a member of the prestigious Domitii Ahenobarbus family, boasting two centuries of consuls, and a dynasty as old as the Roman republic itself. The family *legend* traced the Ahenobarbus, or 'Bronze Beard', name back to the 498BC Battle of Lake Regillus, where *prophecising a victory over the Latins*, the mythological Dioscuri brothers stroked the beard of Lucius Domitius, turning it bronze.

Sejanus may have thought himself very clever, but by targeting the descendants of Augustus, he had reached too far. In a rare moment of clarity, Tiberius had his Prefect ambushed, imprisoned, and strangled to death. Though Sejanus' death offered some relief, it was of little consequence to the elder Agrippina, whose oldest son had already died in prison. Nor was it any consolation to her second-eldest, who remained locked up in a dungeon on Rome's Palatine Hill for two years, before being deliberately starved to death – desperately tearing out the stuffing from his mattress and swallowing it in a futile bid to end his agony. On the second anniversary of Sejanus' downfall, having been left to languish in exile, in a final act of defiance, the heartbroken Agrippina starved herself to death. Rinsing his hands of guilt, Tiberius told the Senate she had killed herself in grief, at the death of a supposed lover.

Amidst the chaos and heartache, desperate for security, the teenage Agrippina the Younger clung perilously to married life. Unfortunately, while her husband Gnaeus served briefly as consul, he was hardly a catch. Asides from being far older, he had a reputation for idleness and frivolity. He was rumoured to have murdered a freedman for not drinking enough alcohol; gouged out a knight's eye for reprimanding him in the middle of the Forum; and even run over a child with his chariot on purpose. The scoundrel was further accused of cheating bankers, and swindling charioteers out of their prize money, until his sister ridiculed him into humility.

Tiberius grew increasingly arbitrary and tyrannical in old age. Like so many others, Gnaeus found himself on the receiving end of his wrath; charged with having an incestuous affair with his sister; only to be spared by the emperor's death in 37. When the Senate appointed Agrippina's brother Caligula to succeed Tiberius, it seemed that Fortuna was again smiling down upon the Julio-Claudians. Ancestral honour was deeply important to the Romans, and Caligula's popularity and prestige were not just bound to that of their father, but the ill-treatment of his family. His rising tide would lift the entire bloodline.

During Tiberius's funeral oration, the new emperor bragged of his descent from Augustus, and the remarkable character of his father Germanicus, before personally carrying the ashes of his mother and brother into the mausoleum of Augustus. His sisters, meanwhile, were made honorary Vestal Virgins, represented as allegorical figures on coins, and mentioned in the preambles to senatorial proposals, the annual vows for the emperors' safety, as well as the annual oath of allegiance to him. They were even allowed to watch the circus games from the imperial seats, the best in the house. In short, they were fully fledged members of the imperial household.

Rounding off this spell of joy, on December 15, Agrippina went into labour at the seaside resort of Antium, described by Cicero as "the quietest, coolest, pleasantest place in the world". Unlike her own auspicious entry to the world, her baby's was an ominous breach birth, considered an "unnatural" and exceptionally dangerous affair. However, from the first sight of her baby, whom she boasted was touched by the rays of the sun at the moment of his birth, something changed in Agrippina. She had purpose.

For a young mother reared on anguish and fear, this boy, the grandson of Germanicus, gave her something to live for. From this moment forth, he would become the focal point of her entire world. Never, she vowed, would he know the terror that had cut short her own childhood, nor let his fate rest in the hands of some fickle tyrant. If Rome was a bed of snakes, she would be an almighty torch, clearing his path towards greatness.

Her perfidious husband was less rather impressed, scowling, "Nothing born of myself, and Agrippina can be other than odious and a public disaster." Her brother, Caligula, had grown increasingly obnoxious in the company of the wretched Tiberius and snidely suggested the boy be named after their uncle Claudius, the lame, disfigured butt of every imperial family joke. Instead, in accordance with Bronze Beard tradition, the boy was named after his grandfather, Lucius. Wondering what the stars might hold for her son, Agrippina consulted an astrologer, who warned that the boy would one day rule Rome. But, to do so, he would have to kill his own mother. Agrippina yelled out in defiance, "Let him kill me, only let him rule!"

Chapter 2: It's a Long Way to the Top

It wasn't long before Agrippina's fragile peace was once again shattered, when Caligula fell gravely ill and began behaving more erratically by the day. Everyone knew Drusilla was his favourite sister; the two were so close, some even suggested that they may have grown too close for comfort. But when the emperor named her his heir in a fevered frenzy, it sent shockwaves across the capital. Suddenly, the rumours of their incestuous liaisons didn't seem so ridiculous anymore.

Although the emperor recovered, his beloved Drusilla fell ill and died the next year, sending him spiralling into a mental breakdown. Before long, the entire empire was engulfed in an avalanche of paranoia, tyranny, and debauchery. Whether truly worried for his own safety or simply a sadist, it didn't take long for the emperor to begin turning on those closest to him, forcing his father-in-law, and heir apparent, the Praetorian Prefect Tiberius Gemellus, to commit suicide.

Quite contrary to Augustus's tactful approach, Caligula seduced men's wives, revived the despotic treason trials, spent a fortune on a vanity bridge across the Bay of Naples and fashioned himself as a living god. Scarcely a corner of the empire remained undefiled by his excess, with even the Temple of Jerusalem instructed to erect a statue of him within its sacred bowels. At one notorious dinner party, sat with the two consuls, the emperor spontaneously burst out laughing. When they asked him what was so funny, he howled, "Just the thought that I would only have to nod, and your throats would be cut on the spot".

These were no idle threats. After executing his brother-in-law, Marcus Lepidus, for conspiring against him, in a fit of paranoia, the emperor turned on his sisters Agrippina and Livilla, accusing them of having sex with the traitor. With no evidence to back his assertion, Caligula simply produced it out of thin air, forging letters in their handwriting, attesting to their treasonous adultery. In a demented parody of her own mother's return from Syria, Agrippina was forced to carry Lepidus' ashes to Rome, before having all her property seized, and being sent into exile. Amidst the carnage, her husband Gnaeus fled the capital with their son, only to die later that year from a fatal case of oedema at Pyrgi, in Etruria, his body swelling up with fluid.

Their three-year-old son, Lucius, meanwhile, was sent to live with his paternal aunt Domitia Lepida. Although Roman law dictated the boy was owed a third of his father's estate, uncle Caligula kept it for himself. However, what Lucius lacked in inheritance, his Auntie Domitia made up for with love and affection. During his stay, Domitia married her own daughter, Messalina, to Claudius, the only adult male member of the Julio-Claudian dynasty that Caligula had allowed to live. Largely because he considered him a joke and enjoyed mocking him so much. Despite Claudius's blue blood, at 30 years Messalina's senior, twice-divorced, physically deformed, and ill-tempered, he was hardly a heartthrob.

On 24 January 41, the tide turned once again, when three disgruntled members of the Praetorian Guard stabbed Caligula to death, before butchering his wife and infant daughter. One of the assassins, Cassius Chaerea, had served as the emperor's chief agent and torturer, only to be repeatedly chastised as "girlie". He was not alone in his fury. In just four short years, the son of Germanicus had caused so much offense, and so thoroughly disgraced his post, that the entire empire now hung in the balance. This was an unprecedented moment.

When the consuls heard what had happened, sensing a unique opportunity to reclaim their lost powers, they scurried about, trying to drum up support for a return to the Republic. Heeding the call, the Senate held an impromptu meeting at the Temple of Jupiter on the Capitoline Hill, the most sacred site in Rome, and the physical embodiment of its endurance. This, some declared, would be the day that Rome overthrew a century of political slavery, ushered in with the triumvirate of Caesar, Pompey, and Crassus. The consul Gnaeus Sentius Saturninus roared out a rousing speech, declaring he had seen "the evils with which tyrannies fill the state", and that the Senate should bestow "the highest possible honours" on Caligula's killers. When one of Saturninus' peers interrupted to yank the signet ring symbolising his loyalty to Caligula off his finger, everyone realised the farcical nature of their efforts. Things were too far gone. The 300,000-strong army was in control now, and for the past 70 years, the legions had been loyal not to the Senate, nor even to Rome, but to the Julio-Claudian dynasty itself.

Augustus had made himself commander-in-chief over Rome's first standing army, and it was he and his descendants who controlled their promotions, term limits and pensions.

When news of Caligula's death reached the Praetorian Guard, all hell broke loose. Overcome by a furious bloodlust for vengeance, the German members of the Guard, loyal to the family of Germanicus, embarked on a violent killing spree, trawling the Palatine, dragging out any noble suspected of being involved and hacking them to pieces. Quivering behind a curtain in an empty room, the craven Claudius felt a hand grip his shoulder. The 50-year-old shook with terror. He was done for.

To his amazement, rather than butchering him, the men hoisted him up, smiled and roared that he was their new emperor. As drunk as they were on revenge, they were sober enough to recognise their fates were intertwined with the imperial system. Having survived the terrors of Sejanus, Tiberius and Caligula, Claudius was the last Julio-Claudian man left standing. As the soldiers paraded him to the Praetorian Camp, the consuls and tribunes desperately tried to intercede, demanding he reject the title and submit to the will of the people. Yet, when their own guards dissolved away, most of the Senate fled to the safety of their country estates, and the futility of their efforts became all too clear.

A meticulous chronicler of history, Claudius stepped into the mould of Augustus and feigned humility; insisting he couldn't possibly accept so great a responsibility. Of course, he was careful not to protest too strongly, just enough to give the appearance that he was acquiescing to the will of the people. More importantly, he handed the Praetorian Guard a massive payout, as a reward for saving his wrinkled skin.

Much to Agrippina's relief, Claudius immediately recalled her from exile, clearing her name and restoring her son's rightful inheritance. A month later, the emperor's wife Messalina bore him a son, who would later be named Britannicus, after Claudius's successful invasion of Britain. Yet, Agrippina was too shell shocked to celebrate. From her earliest memories of her mother carrying her father's ashes to Rome, to her recent spell in exile, she had spent her whole life running along a scorching knife's edge. Security was fleeting, allies scarce and danger constant. Her worst fears were confirmed when her sister Livilla was once again exiled, for supposedly committing adultery with the philosopher and senator, Lucius Amnnaeus Seneca.

Born in around 4BC, the second son of a wealthy family, Seneca was one of Rome's most brilliant philosophers, educated in the School of the Sextii. He embraced the Stoic philosophy, rooted in the idea that everything in existence was governed by a force of supreme reason. The Stoics believed that life should be spent harmonising with this all-encompassing law of reason, and that the highest virtue was the acquisition of knowledge. Whether high or low born, one should accept the natural ebbs and flows of fortune and divorce oneself from emotion in the pursuit of virtue.

After recovering from an illness in Egypt, Seneca

returned to Rome in 31 and made his entry into politics. However, like Agrippina, he fell afoul of Caligula, who only allowed the philosopher to live because he thought he would soon succumb to his illness anyway. Now that Caligula's reign of terror had come to a close, Seneca joined the exodus of exiles, returning to a capital under new management.

Keenly aware of Seneca's ability to sway the Senate with his unrivalled oratory skills, Claudius's wife, Messalina, was terrified that he might lend his abilities to one of her political rivals. So, she accused him of having an affair with Livilla, hoping that the Senate would condemn both to death, killing two birds with one stone.

Messalina's life in many ways mirrored Agrippina's own. Their blood was very much intertwined. The niece of Agrippina's dead husband, she was also the cousin of young Lucius. Two beautiful descendants of Augustus, both in their prime, they were natural rivals. Like Agrippina, Messalina had lost her father at a young age, and knew too well the risks of her bloodline. She may not have loved her hideous, older husband, Claudius, but being Rome's first lady meant safety and stability for her and her young boy, Britannicus. That was something she would not risk for anyone, and now she was on top, she was determined to cut down any ambitious social climbers nipping at her well-worn heels.

Agrippina soon gave Messalina good reason to fear her charms, after convincing her uncle Claudius to have the Senate spare Seneca the death penalty. Instead, Seneca would spend the next eight years in exile on Corsica, where he continued to write philosophy and drama. Though he was keen to return to Rome, he waited patiently, reflecting that "one man's exile was but a drop in the sea of human upheaval".

Like Messalina, Agrippina knew Seneca would make a powerful ally, and how better to secure his loyalty than by saving his life? Sure enough, Messalina was an ambitious, and proficient, schemer, but Agrippina was another beast entirely. Her life had been spent beneath the lingering Sword of Damocles, surviving one psychotic megalomaniac after another. Royal intrigue wasn't just a skill; it was second nature. Messalina didn't stand a chance.

Eager to begin chipping away at Messalina's public standing, Agrippina used Messalina's own machinations as a springboard for an almighty propaganda campaign, smearing her rival as a cold and calculating schemer. She spread nasty stories about the emperor's wife, including one particularly shocking yarn about how the cowardly Messalina sent a group of cretinous assassins to strangle her beloved Lucius in his sleep. The genius of the yarn was that it was rooted in truth; Messalina considered the boy a rival to her own son, Britannicus, and wanted him dead.

According to the tale, the attackers were foiled by an auspicious serpent, which coiled itself around the baby's crib, protecting him. The story spread like wildfire, and Agrippina brilliantly followed it up by placing a snakeskin inside a gold bracelet and making her son wear it at all times, claiming it was the skin of the very beast that had protected him. It was a masterstroke, a constant physical reminder of the boy's divinity, and his potential claim to the throne, as well as the disgraceful ambitions of Messalina.

If it was war Agrippina wanted, it was war she would have. Agrippina may have had Claudius's ear, but Messalina had his bedchamber. At her urging, the emperor ordered Agrippina's exiled sister Livilla to be starved to death. Going a step further, Livilla's husband, the senator Marcus Vinicianus was accused of treason and forced to commit suicide. As Agrippina raced to weave her own webs of alliances across high society, Messalina conspired with Narcissus, one of three imperial freedmen who had become incredibly powerful during Claudius's reign. Narcissus in many ways embodied the undemocratic, arbitrary, nepotistic corruption that plagued Claudius's court.

The imperial bureaucracy Claudius inherited was an incredibly complex behemoth. There were departments for Latin and Greek correspondence, financial accounts, preparing and organising legal cases presided over by the emperor, and even handling petitions. Staffed with hundreds of slaves, they were each managed by freedmen, former slaves, of whose loyalty Claudius could be assured. Although the Senate simmered with rage over the power such lowly people wielded, they daren't voice it.

Every day, the palace overflowed with sacks of letters and an endless flood of envoys, hungry for the emperor's attention. While he had little interest in such menial tasks, Claudius liked to sit in on trials that had traditionally been reserved for other tribunals and joined other advisors when ordinary magistrates took on a case. His tendency to overreach, and bypass the law, made his attention a most valuable asset indeed, and under his administration, the freedmen with his ear sold it to the highest bidders. In this manner, they became some of the wealthiest men in Rome, with the crooked Pallas reported to have amassed a fortune of 300 million sesterces.

Messalina was well aware of the political capital that Claudius's top three freedmen, Narcissus, Pallas and Callistus, held, and was careful to ingratiate them to herself. When she wanted to do away with her stepfather Appius Junius Silanius, it was Narcissus she turned to. The two concocted an absurd plot: one morning, each ran to the emperor, telling him of a horrific nightmare they had in which Silanius had murdered the emperor. Their combined testimony was enough to convince the frivolous Claudius to have the unsuspecting senator executed.

Messalina soon became renowned not just for her ruthless ambition, but her insatiable sexual appetite, and willingness to weaponise it against her enemies. Some claimed she'd only had Vinicianus and Silanius killed because she was bitter they rejected her sexual advances. In the great Roman game of intrigue, she was the most scandalous figure of them all. Courtiers and nobles suppressed gasps as they traded stories of her prominent lovers, one of whom was said to have harboured a foot fetish; and was so obsessed with Messalina's toes, he kept a pair of her shoes with him at all times, compulsively kissing them. But before long, the excitement turned to horror, as the bodies continued to pile up. Other victims included a Praetorian Guard member who threatened to expose her infidelities and Claudius's son-in-law, who was stabbed to death in his bed.

Sensing a dangerous escalation at hand, Agrippina recalled how vulnerable her own mother had been after her father's untimely death. If she was going to stop Messalina from outflanking her, she needed a worthy ally. In Roman society, it was unseemly for a great-granddaughter of Augustus in her mid-twenties to be without a suitable husband. After being rejected by the influential military man, Servius Sulpicius Galba, she set her sights a little closer to home; on her sister-in-law's wealthy husband, Sallustius Passienus Crispus.

Never too bashful to shirk a scandal, she launched a two-pronged attack, unleashing her irresistible charms on the hapless Passienus, while asking Claudius for his support. Passienus' wife Domitia was a formidable lady herself; it was her berating that had compelled her dead brother, Agrippina's late husband Gnaeus, to stop cheating charioteers out of their winnings. However, Crispus simply could not resist. Whether moved by the stick of Claudius, or the carrot of Agrippina, he did as he was asked, divorcing his wife to marry Agrippina.

Becoming consul for a second time in 44, Crispus was a triple threat; prestigious, powerful, and wealthy, a perfect suitor for Agrippina's political ambitions. Asides from funnelling her rumours about Messalina's infanticidal ways through his social network, he named Agrippina and her son as heirs to his alleged 200 million sesterces, making them incredibly rich.

Later that year, Claudius held a special edition of the Secular Games, a series of theatrical spectacles and sacrifices, to commemorate Rome's 800th anniversary. During the ceremony, the nine-year-old Lucius was paraded in public for the first time, riding on horseback during the Game of Troy alongside Britannicus, three years his junior, and the sons of other nobles. To Messalina's horror, Agrippina's son received a more impassioned ovation than her own, which sent her paranoia through the roof. Although she had borne Claudius two children, including a biological heir, she was growing terrified by the threat posed by Lucius and his scheming mother. Meanwhile, her husband's elderly, unpleasant frame only deepened her desire to seek pleasure elsewhere.

Fuelled by fear and passion, her ambition spun out of control, as she embarked on a slew of dangerous liaisons. She was reported to have seduced prominent figures such as Decimus Valerius Asiaticus, the first Gaul to ever win a consulship, who she later convinced Claudius to condemn to execution without trial. Arrested on charges of adultery, bribery, and 'effeminacy', Asiaticus duly cut his wrists, lamenting that had fallen victim to "a woman's guile". A string of political executions and murders followed, with many a scorned lover falling prey to Messalina's violent streak.

She also organised the exile of Claudius's popular and honourable scholar freedman, Polybius, who was eventually executed for crimes against the state; a move that alienated her from the emperor's other powerful freedmen. In this manner, just like the tyrannical latter years of Tiberius's reign, Claudius's court was consumed by what Seneca described as an "epidemic" of closed-door treason trials, where prominent men were executed on a mere whim.

In 47, Messalina finally lost her grip on reality. Tired of her miserable old husband, she allegedly convinced the consul-elect Gaius Silius to leave his wife and marry her. Together, they would overthrow the emperor, place Silius in charge until Britannicus was of age, and live happily ever after. When Claudius left the capital to visit his magnificent new harbour at Rome's port of Ostia, she set her plan in motion.

Despite being legally married to the emperor, Messalina put on a bridal gown and held a wedding ceremony, complete with witnesses and sacrifices. As the matrimonial spilled out into public view, with a hedonistic party and breakfast, the conspiratorial freedman Narcissus sensed the outlandish, delusional scheme was doomed to fail, and wanted to distance himself from it as much as possible. He sent word to Ostia, to tell poor old Claudius what was happening.

The emperor was livid. This was not only a personal disgrace, but high treason. Messalina's downfall was swift. Refusing her the opportunity to wriggle her way out of it, Narcissus, in a grotesquely inappropriate display of his power, took control of the Praetorian Guard and had her and Silius killed. Whether Messalina was truly the murdering temptress she was characterised as, or just a victim of the manipulations of Agrippina and Narcissus, it mattered not. The dead do not write history.

While all of this was going on, Agrippina's wealthy husband rather conveniently dropped dead, leaving both her and her uncle, emperor Claudius, searching for a spouse. In typically corrupt fashion, Claudius's first instinct was to ask his freedmen for recommendations, as if they were his friends or advisors. Naturally, Agrippina emerged as one of the frontrunners. Despite the minor issue of incest, their union seemed like a no-brainer. Besides, when did the Julio-Claudians ever let a little incest get in the way of a good marriage? Although the Senate's blessing was required, they didn't take much convincing, and in 49 Agrippina was married to the most powerful man in the empire.

The day of their nuptials was marked by the suicide of one of Augustus's prominent young descendants, Lucius Junius Silanus Torquatus. Silanus had been set to marry Claudius's daughter, Octavia, which would have throttled him up the imperial pecking order. However, Agrippina wanted to save that honour for her own son and intervened, drumming up trumped up charges Silanus sleeping with his sister. When Silanus' own brother-in-law testified to their incestuous bond, he was stripped of his praetorship and hurled into the political wilderness. With his star extinguished, he ended his life in a great final act of protest against the black hole of power that was Agrippina.

The next year, the 60-year-old emperor adopted Agrippina's son Lucius as a member of the imperial household, despite the danger this posed to his biological son Britannicus's own prospects. On February 25, to commemorate the occasion, Lucius was given a new name: Nero Claudius Cesar Drusus Germanicus. Or Nero for short.

Chapter 3: Mother Knows Best

Agrippina had done it. She was not just the most powerful woman, but one of the most powerful people, in all of the Empire. Within a year of her marriage to Claudius, she became the youngest woman to receive the honorific title of Augusta. Her 13-year-old son, meanwhile, was allowed to dress in the toga virilis of manhood a year early, marking his formal ascent into public life. With bronze hair, deep set eyes, soft ears and a slight chin, the handsome adolescent cut quite a contrast to the unsightly emperor. Coins were even minted, depicting Nero clad in a sharp military cloak, and donated to the soldiers in his name.

He was named Princeps Iuventutis, the Leader of the Youth, and handed the same privileges Augustus's late grandsons Gaius and Lucius had received. The Senate even nominated him consul; despite the fact that he would not enter office for another six years, it was a powerful gesture. On a more practical note, as consul-elect, they awarded him proconsular imperium, or authority, outside the capital, and he was inducted into the four ancient priesthoods.

Amassing fame and adoration, he led the Praetorians in parade and when games were held in his honour, the stark difference between Nero, beaming in his triumphal toga, and Britannicus, in his boy's garb, was lost on no one. Coins minted in the Eastern and Danube provinces depicted Nero on one side and Britannicus on the other, and one African colony struck Nero's face on the reverse. As Britannicus's gleaming mug gradually faded from Roman coinage, his path to the throne became increasingly obscured by the halo of Nero.

In 53, Agrippina formalised Nero's meteoric rise with a prestigious marriage to Claudius's daughter, Octavia. Like Agrippina's marriage to Claudius, Nero's betrothal to his step-sister was a rather lurid arrangement, one that required Octavia to be transferred out of her own family group, which Nero was now a member of, to bypass the technicality of incest. Never wasting a moment's momentum, Agrippina continued to weave her political web, rewarding those perceived as loyal to Nero, while pushing Britannicus's supporters to the sidelines.

Recalling the role the Praetorian Guard had played in murdering Caligula, and appointing Claudius, Agrippina recognised their support had become a crucial part of the emerging succession process. Unfortunately for her, the two Praetorian Prefects in charge of the Guard owed their positions to the machinations of Messalina, and though she was gone, remained fiercely loyal to her son, Britannicus. Unable to wrench them from the pitiful young prince, in another strategic masterstroke, she began eroding their base from the ground up. One by one, she had Claudius remove any centurion or tribune who outwardly showed pity to Britannicus, arguing against the dangers of factionalism. Once the Guard was filled with allies, arguing that having two Prefects encouraged competition and infighting, she remarkably convinced her dour husband to not only remove the two Praetorian Prefect loyal to Messalina, but to replace them with a single Prefect of her choosing.

The man she selected was Sextus Afranius Burrus, a military veteran in his 50s from an equestrian family. The equestrians were essentially the non-political members of Rome's upper class, who derived their names from the hefty cost cavalrymen historically paid to own and maintain their horses. While Augustus required senators to own a whopping one million sesterces to qualify for their rank, equestrians were expected to own 400,000 sesterces. Though senators enjoyed the best seats in the house at public spectacles, and could obviously run for the Senate, the divide between the two was becoming increasingly blurred.

Burrus was the quintessential epitome of the new form of equestrian, a man who, over a long and storied military career, rose through the ranks on the back of his abilities and character alone. After serving as an officer and tribune, he went onto be appointed procurator, a financial agent responsible for managing the emperor's estates. And now, thanks to Agrippina, as the sole Praetorian Prefect, he had become a kingmaker, who was sure to support her son Nero, when the time came.

Agrippina's political triumvirate was completed with the recall of the philosopher Seneca from exile, who owed both his life, and his return, to Agrippina. Although Seneca had earned the right to join the Senate, like Burrus, he hailed from a provincial equestrian family. As a man of unimpeachable moral fibre, he was uniquely ill suited for the path of public life. He believed in moral absolutes, the virtues of the brotherhood of man and universal humanism, values that he had so far always prided himself on abiding. Upon his return, Agrippina not only had Seneca appointed a praetor, or judicial officer, but her son's personal tutor.

Among the finest minds of his time, Seneca was tasked with giving the boy a first-class Greek liberal education and shaping him into a worthy leader. Yet, for a man of immovable morals, it was a precarious situation, and Seneca would have his work cut out for him. Although Nero quickly took to the art of rhetoric, he was rather more interested in the baser pursuits of music and athletics. The boy was simply obsessed with the circus, playing every day with little toy chariots crafted from ivory, a hobby that Seneca considered a waste of energy. The philosopher held the barbaric gladiatorial bouts in particularly low esteem, writing letters to his friends, urging them not to attend blood sports. However, here he was at the centre of Roman power, moulding the mind of the young boy who increasingly looked like he would one day be emperor. As for the other contender, Britannicus, Agrippina appointed another suitable tutor: herself. She personally took over his education, seizing complete control over the young lad.

For her Herculean efforts, Agrippina expected the utmost devotion from her son. She jealously guarded him against the affections of his aunt Domitia Lepida, who had protected him back when his mother was exiled. Lepida had loved Nero even more than her own estranged daughter Messalina and offered him a quiet haven away from the stress of public life; not to mention the constant drone of Agrippina's compulsive, paranoid scheming. Her affection for Nero came at the expense of her own grandson, Britannicus. However, as someone who existed outside of Agrippina's network of influence, Lepida's relationship with Nero naturally represented a threat to the empress, as a possible rival source of influence and control. Agrippina's killer instinct drove her to destroy Lepida with callous precision, accusing her of witchcraft and disturbing the peace by failing to control her herdsmen. In a wicked exercise of power, she even forced Nero to testify against his aunt, sealing her fate. Lepida was promptly executed.

Yet Agrippina could not shield Nero from external influences forever. Every day, the imperial family dined with a vast array of nobles. To Rome's elites, dinner was an important ritual, one that projected prestige, and reinforced a sense of hierarchy. Good hosts would not just woo their guests with exotic delicacies, like ostrich or flamingo, but diligently seat them in accordance with status. Nervously looking from side to side, visitors could assess how they were perceived by the power elites of Rome. Dinner parties also presented courtiers and senators a unique opportunity to influence policy, as well as their own standing. Their children too, were given a chance to brush shoulders with the leaders of tomorrow at the children's table. It was there that Nero first took a liking to the mischievous little rapscallion, known as Otho, whose father had been granted patrician status by Claudius himself.

Asides from these personal relationships, Nero continued to impress the public as Prefect of Rome, judging court cases when ordinary magistrates were away for the Latin festival, and holding games in honour of his stepfather. However, in February 54, Britannicus turned 13, the same age Nero had been allowed to put on the toga virilis. Naturally, Claudius began formalising arrangements for succession planning, and even drafted a secret will. He was now an elderly man, and in pretty poor health at that.

Given how ruthlessly she and Messalina had dealt with rival contenders, the prospect of Nero being overlooked must have terrified the calculating Agrippina. She may have had good reason to be concerned, with some speculating that there was trouble in paradise. Claudius was alleged to have outwardly begun expressing remorse over his increasingly loveless marriage. During a trial of a woman condemned for adultery, he supposedly lamented that he was destined to have wives who were "unchaste, but not unpunished".

However, her worries were short lived. On 13th October, Claudius suddenly fell ill and dropped dead. His mourning widow kept a lid on the news, waiting, quite literally, until the stars aligned in her favour before telling the Praetorian Guard. Finally, when the time was just right, her ally Burrus hauled Nero out of the palace and ushered him to the Praetorian Camp, where he had his men proclaim the teenager emperor. Naturally, remembering the futility of the opposition to Claudius's appointment, the Senate followed suit, handing Nero the tribunician power and proconsular imperium, while lavishing his mother with a fitting array of honours.

It all happened so quickly, no one even thought to consult Claudius's will, but Agrippina had it quashed anyway, just in case it favoured Britannicus. People were starting to sense a pattern form around Agrippina, who now had two husbands drop dead at incredibly opportune moments. Some accounts claimed that Claudius collapsed and suffered an agonising, lingering death over the course of the night. However, the most popular story alleged that Agrippina had her notorious poisoner Locusta prepare a fatal concoction, which was mixed into Claudius' favourite treat, a mushroom, and fed to him by his trusted eunuch food taster. One brutal rumour even claimed that when Claudius vomited the poison up, Agrippina had a toxic enema stuffed up his backside for good measure.

However he died, Claudius was sent off to the afterlife with a grand public funeral, and declared a god by the Senate. During the ceremony, a sombre Nero delivered a flattering panegyric eulogy, penned by his advisor, and propagandist-in-chief, Seneca. Keenly aware of Claudius's shortcomings, Seneca wanted to distance his young protégé from the emperor's excesses, without completely bringing his lineage into disrepute. Nero's entire claim to power was tied to his role as the adopted Son of the Divine Claudius. He was a member of the royal household, and as a Roman, he shared in both the glory and shame of his ancestors. It was a difficult balancing act, one that few but the brilliant Seneca could have executed so masterfully.

Once the mourning period was over, Nero visited the Senate chamber and delivered another of Seneca's orations, thanking the senators and soldiers for their loyalty, and outlining his manifesto. Although less solemn than the last speech, it once again demonstrated a profound level of measure from the young ruler. Despite renouncing Claudius's corrupt and tyrannical excess, he promised amnesty to those who had profited from the worst abuses of power. Yet it was not unity that lay at the heart of this new vision, but one powerful word: clemency.

No more would Rome hold treason trials of prominent figures behind closed doors. Never again would a man be executed based on a mere dream from a scheming wife, and a greedy freedman. This emperor would not allow his advisors to whore his ear to the highest bidder, nor tolerate his wife, freedmen or friends meddling in the affairs of the empire. All of this corruption, Nero asserted, did the Senate, that great noble body, a great disservice. Unlike his predecessor, he vowed that he would happily share his power with the Senate, defiantly booming: "Let the Senate keep its ancient functions; let Italy and the public provinces stand at the judgement seat of the consuls; he would look after the armies entrusted to his care."

Since Augustus, the empire had been divided into various types of provinces. While some of these were imperial holdings, managed by the emperor's appointed military governors or equestrians, the Senate managed 10 provinces on behalf of the Roman people. Nero promised that under his leadership, he would see to his own affairs, and allow the Senate to run its own provinces, without undue imperial influence.

Clemency was one of the most noble Roman virtues, one that Julius Caesar himself had propagandised during his civil wars. When the Senate elevated the first emperor Augustus in 27BC, they erected a gold shield in the Senate House, commemorating the four great virtues of bravery, clemency, justice, and piety. The word clemency was often used in relation to Rome's military conquests, and more recently to symbolise moderation between political enemies, as well as judicial excellence. When Tiberius's political prosecutions grew out of control, the Senate voted to erect an altar of clemency to dissuade him from his tyranny.

This was hardly the first time the Senate had heard an emperor make such promises; Nero's predecessors had reduced them to a mere formality. Claudius himself had vowed to make amends for Caligula's excess and rule with clemency, only to preside over an epidemic of political prosecutions. Seneca held him responsible for the deaths of 35 senators and 221 equestrians.

Yes, it did seem there was something different in the air. The poet Calpurnius Sicilus certainly seemed to think so, singing, "Clemency has broken the frenzied swords. No longer will the fettered Senate in funeral procession weary the executioner. No longer will the wretched Senate chamber be empty and the prison full." Mimicking the feigned humility of Augustus, Caligula and Claudius, Nero postponed his acceptance of the title Pater Patriae, 'Father of the Fatherland', lest he be accused of overreach. He also declined to erect gold and silver statues of his likeness, or even to have the first month of the year changed to the month of his birth. On a more practical note, like Claudius, he handed the Praetorians a generous donation, but rather more extraordinarily, surprised soldiers by making a point of memorising, and greeting them by their, names.

Before long, even the eldest members of the Senate began to feel that in time things really might be different. For starters, Nero began his reign by actually delivering on his promises. He encouraged the Senate to embrace its newfound freedom, by overturning one of his predecessor's most egregious edicts. Claudius used to love muscling his way into cases that should have been adjudicated by other tribunals, sitting among the advisors when ordinary magistrates were in session. With his reliance on corruptible freedmen, this opened up the courts to rampant bribery.

In 47, at the suggestion of Messalina's treasonous lover, Silius, the emperor overturned the Lex Cincia, which banned forensic orators, advocates, and lawyers from accepting money or presents. It was a move that made corrupt figures, like Silius himself, incredibly wealthy, as they exploited hapless clients, charging extortionate fees, only to betray them to the other party for massive bribes, driving many a ruined wretch to suicide. Nero's Senate reinstated the law, bringing this grotesque form of judicial corruption to an end. The Senate also overturned another senatorial decree from the same year, which had made incoming quaestor-elects, or financial agents, responsible for arranging gladiatorial games, putting a price on the position.

Nero's wisdom also seemed to extend to the diplomatic front. Having reached what Augustus considered the empire's natural limits, Rome established a puppet king in Armenia to the east. As a buffer state between the Roman and Parthian Empires, Armenia was an important pawn in the great game; the centre of a constant tug-of-war between the two rivals. Just a few months into Nero's rule, Rome's puppet king was embroiled in an internal power struggle and fled, allowing the country to be taken over by the Persian king's brother, Tiridates. Nero's swift response once again thoroughly impressed the Senate, as he entrusted the subsequent war to the general Corbulo, a highly respected veteran whom Claudius had sidelined. Corbulo found the Eastern soldiers embarrassingly inexperienced, and spent the ensuing years training them, to great effect.

In Seneca and Burrus, Agrippina had clearly created a formidable team. Yet, having spent years cultivating her son's rise to power, as he chipped away at her dead husband's legacy, she began to feel slighted; and, even worse, sidelined. On the surface, she remained more powerful than ever, continuing to assassinate her son's most dangerous rivals. With tireless focus, she forced her former ally, the freedman Narcissus to kill himself, and compelled the Asian procurators to poison the proconsul, Marcus Junius Silanus, a brother of the young royal who committed suicide on her wedding day. Having already dispatched of Silanus' siblings, with Marcus' death, Agrippina snuffed out the last of a prestigious family claiming descent from Augustus.

Agrippina's image even adorned Roman coins, alongside that of her son, whose first codeword for the Praetorian Guardsmen was Optima Mater, 'Best of Mothers'. For the most part, she and her son remained inseparable, and could often be seen wandering around the capital together, with Nero glued to the side of his mother's litter. As a priestess of the new cult of Divine Claudius, the Senate granted Agrippina two lictors; public servants who would normally work for a high magistrate. However, as Nero began to achieve the rare feat of pleasing everyone, she could feel her control over him begin to slip.

Power was a compulsion to Agrippina, a survival instinct. Her internal struggle for influence rapidly spilled out into the public domain. Desperate to retain her monopoly of control, she went as far as to have Nero summon senators to the palace, so she could hide away and listen to their debates. Seneca knew this was dangerous territory; if Nero was seen to be under the thumb of his mother, allowing her to openly assert authority over him, his hard-earned reputation would quickly collapse.

These simmering tensions boiled over in the most unlikely of places, Armenia. When a group of Armenian ambassadors arrived in Rome, Agrippina saw an opening to assert herself in a major way. Armenia was one of her son's most pressing foreign policy issues, and she wanted in on the action. When Claudius was emperor, during public spectacles, Agrippina had always sat on a separate dais from the emperor. However, when Nero met the

Armenian delegates in the Senate chamber, as Agrippina arrived, instead of heading to her own dais, she began shuffling towards Nero's. Seneca and Burrus almost swallowed their tongues in shock, equally awe-struck and horrified by Agrippina's gall. If she sat down alongside the emperor on his own dais, as if she were his equal, or co-empress, his entire reign would be brought into disrepute. Yet, they scarcely wanted to humiliate her, lest they incur her wrath. Desperate to avoid a multi-pronged diplomatic disaster, Seneca acted swiftly, urging Nero to stand up, hurry over to his mother and meet her halfway, physically preventing her from sitting at his own dais without personally disgracing her.

As the year drew to a close, Nero looked forward to the first Saturnalia winter solstice festival of his reign. Although it officially fell on December 17, just two days after Nero's 18th birthday, the festival had grown into a beloved week-long bonanza. With all of Rome's schools, courts and businesses closed, the entire city erupted into chaos; drinking, gambling, feasting, and indulging their every vice all day. Recalling the Golden Age, where Saturn had ruled Italy, and people had no material possessions, the capital was flipped on its head. Noblemen dressed in comfortable Greek table clothes, with the pileus caps customarily worn by slaves placed atop their heads. For a brief moment, social distinctions were cast aside; as masters ate alongside slaves, and in some cases, even served them. While it was traditional to exchange gifts of wax candles, clay statuettes or dolls, modern-minded friends and families had taken to giving one another more luxurious gifts too.

Amidst the farce and fiasco of the Saturnalia, Seneca unveiled his new satirical masterpieces, The Pumpkinification of (the Divine) Claudius, a brutal mockery, contrasting Nero's clemency with the ineptitude of his predecessor. He highlighted Claudius's neglect of proper judicial procedure, the corruption of his court and the inappropriate powers wielded of his freedmen. He even went so far as to have the god Augustus intervene to veto the late emperor's deification. Touching on some of the themes threaded through Nero's accession speech, it was nonetheless controversial enough that it was only performed to a limited audience of elites, who lapped it up with appreciative glee.

Saturnalia banquets were held under the leadership of a "king", responsible for entertaining his court with a series of humiliating, absurd and ridiculous commands for his guests. As the city celebrated the start of a new age, Nero's friends fittingly voted him the king, and roared in laughter when he joked about a Greek proverb: "Mushrooms were the food of the gods, since Claudius was made a god by eating one." He may even have belligerently scowled to Otho at some point that he was nothing like his "cruel" and "idiotic" predecessor. After, drunk and merry, he turned to his younger brother, Britannicus, and hoping to embarrass him, commanded him to sing a drinking song. As Britannicus began screeching in a high-pitched voice, laughter quickly turned to silence, when the boy improvised a sad song, lamenting how he had been dispossessed of his claim to his father's throne.

Chapter 4: The Age of Clemency

As Nero entered his second year of rule, he relied increasingly on the counsel of his advisors Seneca and Burrus, who enjoyed the unofficial distinction of being chief among the amici principis, or 'friends of the prince'. After the Armenian incident, Agrippina had grown increasingly frustrated at her inability to control the incorruptible duo. Like Seneca, Burrus was not respected as one of the military's most incorruptible figures for nothing. Though they owed Agrippina their posts, they both sincerely wanted to rid the empire of its worst Claudian excesses. More importantly, their loyalty was to the emperor. Surely, they were all at least on the same page about that?

Although Seneca's rivals mocked Nero for remaining beneath the yoke of his old tutor, the arrangement suited Nero just fine. The intellectual Seneca and martial Burrus balanced one another perfectly, and their profound experience, wisdom and insight gave Nero some breathing room to explore the lighter side of rulership. As his mother and advisors battled for influence, the young princeps, or 'leader', began to fall under the spell of yet another, rather less appropriate, influence. While he happily played the part of dutiful emperor during the day, come dusk, like any noble in his prime, it didn't take much for Otho and the other wild courtiers to lure Nero from the sanctity of the palace.

Under the cloak of night, Nero and his friends dressed up as slaves and hurtled themselves rapaciously through Rome's most notorious brothels, taverns, and low-eating houses, frequented by only the dregs of plebian society, with no space or means to prepare their own food. Most nobles, who took the privilege of being able to cook at home for granted, would never dream of stepping foot in any such disgraceful establishment. They imagined the capital's bars, cafes and restaurants as dark and seedy dens filled with rowdy bandits, sailors, fugitive slaves, coffin makers, and all manner of undesirable rapscallions, brutishly chucking dice and fists at one another.

For most Romans, eating out was a part of life. Some quick dine-and-dash establishments, or thermopolia, featured a streetside counter, hawking bread, cheese, fruit, and vegetables to those in a hurry. Inside, the walls were decorated with fantastical scenes depicting life in the bar itself, while sausages and other treats hung from the ceiling, hovering over vats of wine. Waiters scurried back and forth topping up cups, taking orders, and trying to cool down heated arguments over intense games of dice. Occasionally, drunken customers might scream bloody murder, accusing staff of watering down their wine too much. While others quietly haggled with prostitutes in shady corners.

Nero and his friends lived for such lowly thrills. As they stumbled drunkenly through the narrow, claustrophobic alleyways of Rome's notorious Milivan Bridge area, Otho would chastise Nero for not spending enough money, and challenge him to increasingly ostentatious displays of extravagance.

As time went on, their chaotic exploits took on an air of danger, as Nero and his friends formed a gang, breaking into houses and shops and pillaging them. Any poor soul who crossed their path were manhandled and molested, and if they resisted, beaten to a pulp and hurled into the sewers. One night, a man of senatorial rank defended himself so capably, the emperor was forced to spend days hiding out, applying ointment to his two black eyes. When the two bumped into each other in the light of day, recognising Nero as the emperor, the nobleman fell to his knees apologising, but was pulled aside and compelled to commit suicide. Thereafter, Nero's late-night escapades were trailed by a stream of burly gladiators and guards, standing by in case of emergency. Of course, Nero asked them not to get involved unless invited. Continuing to raise the stakes, Otho invented a cruel sport of wrapping people in blankets, before beating them up. Such incidents hardly screamed 'clemency', but everyone was happy to overlook them; it was just what young nobles did.

The emperor's exploits spilled out into his beloved theatre, where he developed a nasty knack for blurring the line between art and life. From the balcony, to the joy of the plebs, he encouraged pantomime actors to become increasingly violent, inciting full-blown pitched battles. Offering impunity and rewards, he kicked the soldiers out of the theatre and, leading by example, hurled stones and pieces of furniture down onto performers below. The emperor laughed manically as the crowd broke out into almighty riots, and on one occasion, personally left a praetor with a serious head injury. Things grew so out of hand, pantomime actors ended up banished from Italy for four years, and the soldiers were brought back into theatres. Again, while the nobles might not have approved of Nero's childish antics, they did not pose a serious threat to public order, and more importantly, the plebians loved it.

Agrippina, however, was not amused. Although she could overlook such superficial escapades, when her son began cavorting with a young freedwoman called Acte, this was something she would not tolerate. Although Nero had been adopted by Claudius, he owed much of his legitimacy and popularity to his wife, Octavia. Octavia was not only beloved by upper nobility and lower plebians alike but was the great-granddaughter of her namesake, Augustus's own sister, Octavia. Even if the two had no meaningful bond, it was important that Nero was seen to be a good husband to her.

Agrippina was furious at her son's disgraceful conduct. She had worked too hard to secure that marriage for him to squander it on a common freedwoman, no less. This was not just a public humiliation of her beloved daughter-in-law, it was something she took as a personal slight, an act of great disobedience. Gods be damned if she loses her own influence to a nobody like Acte. Enraged, she paced about the palace, ranting, and yelling about having an "ex-slave as her rival and a servant girl as her daughter-in-law" to any who would listen.

Tensions between her and her son simmered, boiling over from time to time, as she took her anger out on his servants, dismissing some and violently beating others. Seeing red, on one occasion she scolded Nero so severely, he immediately cut her off. Terrified, sensing she had transgressed the waning limits of her influence, she immediately changed her tune, offering Nero her vast hoard of wealth, and showering him constant praise.

Ever stoic, Seneca watched on from the sidelines. He knew Agrippina's efforts were in vain. Nero had neither desire nor love for his wife and was clearly bound to stray from her. If anything, this was an opportunity to further break Agrippina's grip over her son, and it was better the emperor concentrated all his lust on Acte, than scandalised the wives of nobles, like Caligula had done. Seneca pulled Acte aside and did what he did best; he prepared a speech for her.

After some coaching, Acte sprinted into Nero's chamber and told him that his mother had been boasting loudly of her influence over him. If he allowed it to continue, she warned, the soldiers would soon lose all respect for him. With that, Nero was sufficiently seduced, and embarked on a long-standing affair with the freedwoman. Seneca rounded off his strategy with an ingenious twist, by having his friend Annaeus Serenas, the Prefect of the Watch, cover up for the emperor, pretending it was he who was sleeping with Acte.

For Nero, this was no mere lurid affair. He was so infatuated with Acte, he set her up as a second-class wife, through an illegal union known as a contubernium. Due to her lowly status as a former slave, during the ceremony, Nero had his friends swear that she had descended from the old kings of Pergamum in Asia Minor.

Although he continued to maintain cordial relations with his mother, it was not to last. She was livid. When the emperor sent her a robe and some jewels that had belonged to some earlier princesses, she complained that he was merely handing her a fraction of what was once all hers. Insulted, the emperor shot back by firing his mother's ally, and the last of Claudius's three powerful freedmen, the financial secretary Pallas. Tellingly, before leaving, Pallas swore himself out of office, as if he were a magistrate. His sacking pushed Agrippina over the edge.

She began to roam the palace and city, roaring that Claudius's biological son, Britannicus was nearly of legal age and that her own son Nero was a mere pretender, who misused his power by attacking his poor beloved mother. Shockingly, she even threatened to present Britannicus to the Praetorian Guard and have them proclaim him emperor. With the sole Praetorian Prefect Burrus firmly in Nero's camp, this was a hollow threat, but for Nero, it was too dangerous to ignore. From Britannicus's miserable song at previous year's Saturnalia festival, he knew that his stepbrother also felt that he'd been disinherited from his birthright.

On February 12, Britannicus was just a day shy of his 14th birthday, when he would finally come of age. Throughout the palace, spirits were high, as the guests gathered for a hearty feast. But as the slaves dished out portions of food to Nero, Agrippina, Octavia and the other nobles, suddenly a commotion broke out across the children's table. Britannicus stood up, desperately grasping at his throat, and began choking, gasping, wheezing, eyes bulging, knocking over his drink. Agrippina's jaw dropped in horror; she knew a poisoning when she saw one. Her eyes darted over to her son, who looked on, stone-faced, callously remarking that his brother must be having an epileptic fit. Octavia ran over to her sibling, weeping, and watching helplessly as his agonising convulsions subsided into death upon the cold floor. It was the perfect crime. Nero gave his mother a look that said it all: the student had become the master.

Even if Seneca or Burrus had been opposed to the move, they didn't vocalise it. They both knew well that Agrippina had played a dangerous game, one that had threatened the life of the emperor, and the stability of the empire itself. Nero rewarded their loyalty with expensive gifts, properties and, most importantly, his attention. His mother, for all her flaws, had picked his counsel wisely, and he was grateful for it. Agrippina, meanwhile, just couldn't let sleeping dogs lie. With Britannicus dead, she continued to rile up senators and members of the Praetorian Guard, over Nero's disgraceful behaviour towards Octavia. This was too much. Nero was fed up. He stripped her of her Praetorian and German bodyguards and kicked her out of the palace, leaving her completely vulnerable to her enemies. And her enemies were many.

Chief among them was Junia Silana, a former friend who she had fallen out with over a man. Smelling blood, Junia accused Agrippina of plotting to overthrow Nero with Rubellius Plautus, a great-grandson of Tiberius, and hence a descendant of Augustus in the same degree as the emperor himself. Nero was informed of the alleged plot by the acclaimed pantomime, Paris.

Given his mother's recent behaviour, it hardly surprised him that she might be capable of infanticide. In fact, it terrified him. His initial reaction was to simply have her killed like Britannicus, but Burrus pushed back. Reminding the emperor of his vows, in typically terse fashion, the Praetorian stickler insisted Agrippina must be given a fair trial. After listening to her defence, he and Seneca suggested Nero interview her personally. Remarkably, the emperor walked out of the conversation so convinced of his mother's innocence that he had her accusers banished, and some even killed instead.

Having once again survived the intrigue, Agrippina managed to steal back some political capital from Seneca and Burrus. When Burrus had gone to interview Agrippina, Nero sent some of his freedmen to listen in and spy on them, indicating a hint of suspicion. Immediately after Agrippina's vindication, Burrus found himself accused of plotting with the freedman Pallas to overthrow Nero. His accusers claimed he wanted to replace the emperor with Faustus Cornelius Sulla Fenix, the husband of Claudius's other surviving daughter Antonia. Nero's trust, however, remained steadfast. He stood by his Praetorian ally, who remained on the emperor's advisory consilium for the proceedings not involving his own defence, and instead enjoyed the satisfaction of seeing his accuser punished instead. Yet, the dynamic duo could see their influence beginning to wane. Nero was becoming his own man, and while his advisors had previously been able to keep his worst excesses in check, allowing him to indulge them was the price they now had to pay to keep his ear.

Ever since he was a boy, Nero had been obsessed with the circus. But, then again, who wasn't? Everyone loved a good spectacle, and the games played a crucial political role in the empire. As a matter of convention, it offered the Roman people a rare opportunity to air their grievances directly to the emperor, without fear of reprisal. It was an unwritten rule that one could say things within the theatre, circus or arena that would not be accepted elsewhere, referred to by Tacitus as 'theatrical license'. Whether they wished to complain about taxes, laws, food shortages or even just to mock the private lives of famous figures, it played a bizarrely democratic function. Spectators could directly ask the emperor to free a beloved gladiator, fire a hated courtier or lower food prices.

Most of the empire's 50 million inhabitants were peasant small farmers, who grew barely enough to feed themselves, sometimes producing a tiny surplus to sell. Rome itself was riddled with urban poverty and decay. Immigrants flocked to the city seeking opportunity, alongside runaway slaves; only to find themselves squatted in the grand aristocratic tombs that lined the entrance to the city. The capital's outskirts were ringed by shantytowns, overflowing with hungry beggars and labourers.

The vast majority of Romans were plebians, or 'plebs'; a working-class of ordinary, industrious, poor people, who were the free citizens of Rome, far beneath the elites.

However, the social ladder was not just long but wide. The lower echelons of the plebs were people with no trade or skills, who worked in bars, construction, restaurants, brothels or at the ports, whenever the opportunity arose. There was plenty of work for day labourers; Rome's one million residents consumed enough oil, wine, and grain to keep 3,000 porters working for 100 days, unloading ships and bringing it to shore. However, these seasonal workers slept in shared rooms in hostels, and never had the luxury of enjoying Rome's many remarkable spectacles.

Most 'ordinary' plebians lived in massive apartment blocks called insulae, or 'islands'. Owned by wealthy landlords, and prowled by ruthless rent collectors, these were physical embodiments of the hierarchy within plebian society. The apartments closer to the ground floor were larger and more luxurious, with access to cooking and washing facilities. Those higher up, meanwhile, were smaller and cheaper, but lacked fire escapes, and basic facilities.

Rome's elites were disgusted by wage labour, which they associated with servility, but for the common pleb, one's job was their identity, a way of life. Unlike the wealthy minority, unable to read or write, they needed regular income to feed their families, and worked from womb to tomb, trying to amass what fortune they could. While wealthy kids spent their days studying rhetoric, philosophy and oratory, poor children as young as four-year-olds might be put to work in the mines. Rome was a diverse and dynamic place, with more than 200 types of jobs available. It needed dyers of 'purple'; the expensive dye extracted from shellfish that only the emperor and senators were allowed to wear, as well as staff for its many bars, cafes and restaurants.

These jobs were exhausting, and often rather fruitless. If they were robbed, they would often have to resolve the issue themselves, hiring vigilantes or even fortune tellers in search of justice. Because their lives were so hard and weary, the plebs loved spectacles. Augustus himself had instituted Rome's pseudo-socialist policy of 'bread and games'; giving the poor people enough free food and entertainment to keep them from rioting. The games offered the plebs an escape from their otherwise mundane, and often depressing, lives.

As such, it was fine for Nero to maintain a passing interest in the spectacles. In fact, Seneca encouraged Nero to put on games; he knew well how important they were to the plebs. It was his duty as emperor to entertain the masses, and perhaps organising a few good shows might help excise the prince of his fixation, most unbecoming a man of the purple robe. Unfortunately, his fixation transgressed mere curiosity; it was a downright obsession. Despite Seneca's best efforts, it was one of Nero's inherent passions he just couldn't stamp out. The man never missed a race, no matter how insignificant, and kept on increasing the prize winnings as a show of appreciation. He reserved particular passion for his favourite team, the Greens, and was able to engage in the most detailed chariot banter with the common plebs, with natural ease. In this way, he was quite unlike any emperor that had come before, and the most beloved among the masses.

More worryingly, he came from a long line of showmen. His grandfather Lucius had scandalised the Roman world by staging farcical pantomimes starring Roman knights and married women. A passionate charioteer, Lucius's beast-baiting and gladiatorial spectacles were so gruesome, Augustus himself personally scolded him and handed him a legal injunction to put an end to them. Lucius's son, Gnaeus, meanwhile, was another racing afficionado, notorious for swindling charioteers out of their prize money.

Now it was Nero's turn to put on a spectacle of his own. Organised by the knight, Arruntius Stella, it was a pretty standard event; one man hunted bulls on horseback, cavalrymen slew hundreds of bears and lions with javelins and 30 knights clashed in an epic gladiatorial battle. By Roman standards, it was a fairly modest affair, perfectly in keeping with Nero's promise of clemency. However, he had also begun to indulge his other Hellenic passions, chiefly his love of music.

The young emperor summoned the world's most accomplished citharode, or lyre player, Terpnus, to his court. After dinner, he spent many an evening watching and listening to the master musician, studying his fingers, while practicing his scales and techniques over and over. He displayed remarkable devotion; determined to become Rome's finest singer, he would lie down for hours with lead plates on his chest and avoided any food that might compromise his throat. On some days, he ate nothing but chives soaked in oil. Of course, he knew to keep such things secret. Among the nobles, it was fine to practice a hobby in private, but it was not a good look for an emperor to pay much attention to so unworthy a pursuit.

However, not all such endeavours had to be hidden. The emperor was comfortable reciting his poems to nobles in private, and the plebians were invited to watch him exercise on the Campus Martius. A lover of Greek athletics, he took his physical fitness seriously, and after particularly intense physical workouts, would drink boar's dung mixed in water. Though exercising was harmless enough, Seneca could hardly hide his disdain for the "groans and gasps" of brawny men exercising "with their lead weights" at the public baths.

Keen to remind the emperor of his imperial commitments, the philosopher penned a treatise called De Clementia. It began: "I have undertaken to write about clemency, Nero Caesar, that I may serve as a kind of mirror and give you the supreme pleasure of seeing your own image." He described clemency as the most commendable quality in men and rulers, a quality that was embodied by the emperor, himself. The treatise rehashed the key pledges of Nero's manifesto: "Profound and deep security, justice elevated above all violation; before their eyes is the joyous spectacle of a form of government that lacks no element of absolute liberty except the licence to be destroyed."

Seneca also highlighted the importance of Rome's dictatorial principate, propagandising the virtue of obedience to the rule of the emperor, lest "unity, this fabric of mightiest of empires... shatter into pieces". Rome, he argued, may have cast off its monarchs long ago, but if the empire was to hold together, it needed an absolute ruler; albeit one who behaved as if he were obliged to obey the laws. "For Caesar and the state have for so long been intermingled that they cannot be separated without the destruction of both; for while a Caesar needs strength, the state needs a head." The treatise went so far as to absolve the emperor of Britannicus's death, and even speculate that perhaps he might one day surpass Augustus.

On the surface, it certainly seemed so. Nero was remedying the ills of Claudius's corrupt regime at a remarkable rate. When a corrupt quaestor, or financial agent, was found guilty of overcharging when collecting debts, Nero reversed the Claudian practice of appointing public officials to run the treasury, and reverted to the Augustan model of using Prefects, who had previously served as a type of magistrate known as the praetor. Furthermore, after a trial where the accuser was exiled for malicious prosecution, the emperor ordered the destruction of debts owed to the treasury had been exploited for profit.

Unlike Caligula, who referred to his monthly authorisation of executions as "clearing his accounts", when signing death warrants, Nero lamented, "How I wish I had never learned to write". But while he restored some decision-making to the Senate, he still took some decisions for the entire realm. For example, in 57 he issued an empire-wide edict banning provincial governors and procurators from holding their own gladiatorial games.

Continuing to project his imperial power, he not only established colonies at Capua and Nuceria, in Campania but sent an expedition of two centurions to Ethiopia, to discover the source of the Nile, mirroring Alexander the Great's commitment to military reconnaissance and studying the natural world. Back in Rome, he built a magnificent wooden amphitheatre on the Campus Martius in under a year. It was the embodiment of prestige, with stone foundations clad in marble, and its main structure surmounted by an awning decorated like the sky, studded with stars.

There, he held a great spectacle, where, again projecting clemency, he forbade participants from killing one another. Instead, he won over the crowd by flooding a theatre with water, filling it with exotic marine life and staging an epic sea battle between the 'Persians' and the 'Athenians', portrayed by nobles. After, the theatre was drained, to allow hundreds of senators and knights to duke it out in individual and group gladiatorial battles, against man and beast alike. While the 19-year-old emperor normally just watched from a private box, this time he personally presided over the games. The poet Calpurnius Siculus, a diehard Nero fanatic, enthusiastically celebrated the grandiose effect of ivory and gold trimmings, with one elderly Roman musing, "All the shows we saw in former years now seem shabby to us".

When the games were over, Nero announced his first ever public largess, handing out a whopping donation of 400 sesterces to every citizen, at a gargantuan cost of 180,000,000 sesterces, or roughly one third of the triumphal donative Augustus had given his veterans from his Egyptian spoils. At the start of 58, Nero followed up by granting the first of a new series of annual subsidies to down-and-out nobles. More importantly, he did so with grace. In the past, when senators came to Tiberius to ask for subsidies, he utterly humiliated them, with Seneca remarking, "It does not befit the principes to inflict humiliation". Nero, on the other hand, refused to insult these proud men by scrutinising what had led them to poverty. His grants were incredibly generous, reaching up to 500,000 sesterces each. He also became the first emperor to grant annual pensions rather than a capital sum.

One of his more ambitious plans centred around tax collection. During the Republic, Rome contracted out the collection of provincial taxes to non-political members of the upper class known as publicani. This tendering process was designed to secure the highest fee possible for the contract, which went straight into the treasury. Private tax farmers would then go and recoup their purchase price from the provincials and keep any surplus. Governors were supposed to make sure the publicans were not over-charging, but the system was open to bribery, corruption, and abuse. As part of his tax reform, Augustus abolished tax farming for direct provincial taxes, but Nero remained inundated with complaints about excessive farming of harbour dues and other indirect taxes.

Moved by accounts of suffering and exploitation, Nero floated the absurd idea of abolishing all indirect taxes. It was an unfathomably grand gesture, one he genuinely hoped would alleviate a great deal of suffering. However, he was soon reminded that this was simply impossible. Though his vision was too much too soon, instead he issued an edict, telling provincial governors and the urban praetor at Rome to give precedence to all cases against such abusive tax farmers. Moreover, he ordered all localities to publicly display indirect tax laws, which were previously obscured or hidden in jargon, so local taxpayers were aware of their rights.

Even as he acted with imperial authority, as promised, Nero continued to share his responsibility with the Senate. On one occasion, when a senator failed to settle the grievances of the population of Puteoli, Nero was brought in to mediate the matter. However, rather than issuing his own decision, he loaned a Praetorian cohort to the two senators sent to follow up. He did, however, intervene on behalf of two proconsuls being prosecuted in Africa, shielding them from justice. But the Senate appreciated the gesture; it was not in their interests to see their peers punished based on evidence submitted by subjects, lest it happen to them.

When Nero's chosen general, Corbulo, achieved a stunning victory in Armenia, driving out the Parthian prince Tiridartes and installing a Roman puppet king, Tigranes, the Senate were simply blown away. Yet, for Seneca and Burrus, there was a new problem on the horizon. Nero had fallen in love again. And, this time, it was not with an obscure freedwoman.

Chapter 5: The Ides of March

Being one of the emperor's friends certainly had its perks, especially for his favourite partner-in-mischief, Otho. When the emperor learned that his drinking buddy was madly in love with a beautiful young married woman, he committed the full weight of the empire to helping him woo her. Using his raw imperial power, he simply had the lady divorced from her husband, and married to Otho instead. Otho could scarcely hide his gratitude, babbling incessantly about his remarkable bride.

Her name was Poppaea Sabina, and she had lived a life of intrigue. Her father had risen from non-senatorial ancestry to become a quaestor, only to end up being forced to commit suicide as an accomplice of Sejanus. His tarnished legacy compelled Poppaea to adopt the name of her maternal grandfather, a modest figure who nonetheless received the consulship and triumphal decorations, serving as governor of Moesia for 24 years.

The Poppaea family were one of the wealthiest and most powerful in Pompeii, and proud owners of several properties, including the esteemed House of the Golden Cupids and the House of Menander. Poppaea's mother, meanwhile, killed herself in prison, after being accused by Messalina of committing adultery. However, she passed on her stunning looks to her daughter. Otho was infatuated with her, even if she'd already had a son with her ex-husband, Rufrius Crispinus, one of the Praetorian Prefects

Agrippina replaced with Burrus.

Though she was six years Nero's senior, he too was taken by her beauty, charm, and intellect. And the more Otho bragged of his bride, the more Nero himself longed for her. It seemed the feeling was mutual. Poppaea flirted ferociously with the emperor, playing him and his best friend against one another in a dangerous competition for her affection. Though, it was hardly a fair fight. In yet another remarkable abuse of power, Nero had his friend appointed the governor of distant Lusitania, in western Iberia, a role that he was at least a decade too young for. With Otho confined to the furthest reaches of the empire, Nero and Poppaea began to openly flout their desire for one another, once again to the fury of Agrippina.

With both of her parents losing their lives to politics, Poppaea understood the intricacies of power. She knew well that despite her respectable origins, she was no match for the daughter of Claudius; Agrippina would never allow her son to divorce Octavia for her. She also recognised that entering a head-on collision with Agrippina would be a battle to the death, and the emperor's mother had never lost a bout yet. As the cold war turned hot, Poppaea weaponised Nero's lust for her, using her overwhelming influence over the emperor to slowly poison him against his mother. He didn't take much coaxing.

Having grown into the role of emperor, Nero was sick of his mother's incessant nagging. As her son drifted further away than ever before, a desperate Agrippina stepped up her game. When she visited him, she did so at noon, when she knew her son was drunk, well-fed and in good cheer.

She presented herself in beautiful makeup and dress, smothering him in kisses and affection. To those around, it was incredibly uncomfortable; it looked like Agrippina had run out of options, and was now trying to seduce her own son. The rumours were not totally groundless; Nero was known to parade around one of his favourite courtiers, who looked exactly like Agrippina, joking that he was having sex with his mother.

Whether Nero and his mother really were sleeping together, Seneca knew Agrippina well enough not to put anything past her. He and Burrus didn't really care if Nero wanted to have sex with Acte, while Otho was nowhere in sight. His own mother, though? They shuddered at the thought. Once again, Seneca sent in his secret weapon of mass distraction, Acte. Though she was no longer Nero's favourite, she held a special place in his heart. So, when she warned him that his mother's seemingly incestuous manoeuvres were putting him in grave danger, he listened. She reminded him of the various times Agrippina had threatened to overthrow him, the threats on his life, and all her attempts to publicly undermine him. With these latest developments, things were getting out of hand. Agrippina had to go.

The last time Nero asked Burrus about killing his mother, the Prefect Praetorian insisted she be given a fair trial. This time, it was not so much a question of whether she should be killed, but how. His mind already made up, Nero came to Burrus not for advice, but for his assistance. Although he made no effort to talk Nero out of it, Burrus bluntly told him he couldn't ask the Praetorian Guard to do it, when so many of them owed their positions and fortunes to her. This was something the emperor would have to do on his own.

Unable to depend on his two most trusted advisors, the emperor turned to one of his old tutors, Anicetus; a freedman who Nero had helped appoint the commander of the fleet at Micenum, at the northwest end of the Bay of Naples. He was a rare figure who owed his lot entirely to the emperor, rather than his mother. Perhaps with a tinge of irony, Nero's instinct was to simply have his mother poisoned, but there was no one bold enough to even dare try.

For the assassination to be successful, Nero would need to simultaneously outwit his mother, while avoiding any responsibility for her death. Murdering one's own mother was an act of unthinkable cruelty, completely contrary to the oldest and most enduring Roman virtues. It was about as low as one could sink. Together with Anicetus, he devised a spectacularly ludicrous plot to out scheme Rome's greatest schemer, as absurd as it was ingenious. They would design a booby-trapped boat, designed to collapse mid-journey, dragging Agrippina to a watery grave. With a nod of agreement, the boat was built and the plot set in motion.

Nero planned to kill his mother just after the Ides of March, at one of the most beloved of the Bay of Naples' resort towns, Baiae. One after another, great palatial villas curved along the shore of the Bay, rising over the hills, and looming over the piers, overlooking the pristine water. This was where Rome's busiest aristocrats and oligarchs escaped to, whenever fortune offered the opportunity. As one popular phrase had it, "No bay in the world outshines delightful Baiae", that "golden shore of blessed Venus, Baiae the seductive gift of proud nature".

Nobles feasted and drank to great excess, and beaches came alive with music and dancing, as formality gave way to hedonism. The pungent aroma of sulphur wafted over from the local hot springs and liquored up stragglers stumbled along the docks in search of pleasure. In the distance, drunks fell from ships and belly-flopped into the sea, while on the shore, Romans ripped off their Greek togas, as beach parties erupted into wild orgies.

Of course, Seneca found the whole scenario fairly grotesque, but Nero loved it. In this case, the capital's finest had come to celebrate the festival of Quinquatria, a celebration of Minerva, the goddess of arts, crafts, martial prowess and medicine. When Nero invited Agrippina to celebrate the occasion with him at his villa in Baiae, she breathed a sigh of relief. Perhaps, she thought, her son had finally come to his senses. As her ship pulled up to the shore, her heart skipped a beat; Nero was waiting at the dock to greet her.

They enjoyed a wonderful dinner together, Nero displaying uncharacteristic vulnerability, laughing louder than usual at her vicious jokes, and starting longingly in those moments of silence between, with tears in his eyes. After dinner, Agrippina sank into her chair, suitably plied with wine and food. It had been a Quinquatria to remember. Minerva had brought her son back to her. As the evening drew to a close, Nero clamped his arms around his mother in a feverish embrace, kissing her eyes and holding her for an eternity, while expressing his undying gratitude.

After, he walked her down to the shore, pointing out the stars that hung over the warm and still air. Spring was well on its way. As they approached the sea, they remarked how serene it looked, and Nero carefully helped his mother onto the ship that he himself had travelled on from Rome. The emperor watched as his mother sailed into the distance, waving and smiling. Smiling back at his fading figure, Agrippina was suddenly jolted to her senses. Wood began to creak and split, exploding all around as the crew were hurled and sucked down into the depths of the sea. Agrippina scarcely had time to think, as she dodged splinters and shrapnel. Her body was thrown aboard, battered, and bludgeoned. Yet, remarkably, as she floated up from the wreckage, summoning what strength she had left, gasping, she dragged her body to the shore and crawled onto dry land.

Pushing through a crowd of stunned onlookers, she stumbled into her villa and fell into a chair in shock; her son had just tried to kill her. Her own son. And yet, he had failed. Determined to kill him with kindness, she sent a freedman messenger to let the prince know that she had miraculously survived a tragic accident, but that she wished to be left alone to recover. Nero had already heard the news. It cut through him like a knife. What now? Would his mother raise an army of slaves, or perhaps even the Praetorian Guard, against him? Would she tell the Senate what had happened? Poison him? Panicking, he summoned Seneca and Burrus, and as they arrived, panting, he paced the room, asking if the Guard would finish the job for him. Burrus scowled, "The guard will commit no crime against a descendant of Germanicus. Let Anicetus fulfil his promise!" As the prince ran off, Burrus shot Seneca one of those looks that said more than one of the philosopher's great orations ever could. This had better work.

Anicetus, of course, was happy to oblige. This was a tremendous opportunity for him. As he excused himself, Nero proclaimed his glee that, with his mother dead, he would finally receive the empire at the hands of a former slave. While Anicetus slipped out, Agrippina's messenger arrived. Without missing a beat, Nero hurled a sword at the man's feet and yelled to his guards that the man was an assassin, sent by his mother to murder him.

Meanwhile, in less theatrical fashion, Anicetus and his ruthless band of sailors burst into Agrippina's villa and barged into her chamber. Onlookers screamed and gasped. True to form, Agrippina chastised their rude entrance, and asked whether they had come to check on her, or to kill her. As the men drew nearer, surrounding her, she had her answer. Without warning, pain burst its way through her skull like a lightning bolt, as one of the marines smashed her over the head with a club. She fell to her knees, with hot blood streaming down her face, and looked up to see a centurion reluctantly raise his sword. A million thoughts raced through her mind, but none presented an opportunity to spin her way out of this situation. She remembered the prophecy, all those years ago; her life flickered before her eyes. Furious, she thrust her womb forwards and roared, "Strike my belly!" The men set upon her with extreme violence, bludgeoning, stabbing, and hacking her to death. The prophecy was fulfilled.

When Nero came to observe his mother's mutilated body, rather than look away, he undressed her and cleaned up her wounds, lamenting, "I did not know that I had so beautiful a mother". He sunk into a deep, dark pit of grief and guilt; he had murdered his mother in cold blood and plain sight. Now all he could to was flee to Naples and hope Rome believed his version of events. Fortunately for the emperor, his mother's reputation preceded her. When word of his brush with death spread to the capital, the public rejoiced. They were just happy that Nero had survived. As far as they were concerned, Agrippina's death was justified. In Naples, while Nero paced his villa, Seneca did his best to calm the storm, frantically writing a letter from Nero to the Senate, formally outlining the official story. His letter painstakingly explained how Agrippina had sent a messenger with a sword to kill the emperor but committed suicide when her plot was foiled.

He dragged up all the dirt he could muster; accusing her of trying to usurp imperial powers for herself, refusing the Roman people their customary donations, of daring to enter the Senate to receive foreign embassies, and even dredging up the many crimes committed during the reign of Claudius. Although far from his finest work, as Seneca listed out Agrippina's various shortcomings and crimes, he did enough to sufficiently smear her name. With a touch of theatrics, bemoaning his cruel fate, his 'Nero' decried,

"I cannot yet believe or rejoice that I am safe".

While Nero's friends gave their heartfelt thanks to the gods at the temples in Rome, Burrus frantically drummed up support in Campania, prompting several towns to offer sacrifices on his behalf, and send envoys congratulating his daring escape. The Senate, too, decreed that thanks should be offered at every shrine and, symbolically, at Agrippina's funeral, Burrus had the Praetorian centurions and tribunes congratulate the emperor. Henceforth, the festival of Minerva would be commemorated with a series of games, in honour of the emperor's safe brush with death, and a statue of the goddess placed next to one of Nero outside the Senate.

The Arval Brothers, a senatorial priestly college, offered two sacrificed on Nero's behalf, with the second offering made to Mars the Avenger in the Forum of Augustus. The wicked Agrippina's birthday would be thrown onto a list of 'unhallowed' days, when no public business could be conducted. Hammering home the point, Nero recalled many of his mother's enemies from exile before finally, three months after her death, sheepishly returning to Rome, to a hero's welcome.

Of course, there were some rumblings of dissent. One night, vandals placed a leather sack over one of the emperor's statues, a reference to the standard punishment for parricide; being drowned in a sack, alongside a snake, cock, and dog. On another occasion, a baby was hurled into the Forum with a placard, reading "I will not raise you and you will not kill your mother". Although every effort was made to remove all of Agrippina's statues as quickly as possible, it was too slow to stop her fans from dressing one of them in rags, with an inscription: "I am ashamed, and you are not". There were bad omens too. When the Senate was offering sacrifices, there was a total eclipse of the sun, and on one occasion, as elephants drew the chariot of Augustus into the Circus, they stopped in front of the senators' seats, refusing to go any further. Nero's own dining table at his villa in Subicao was supposedly struck by lightning.

As the emperor walked the streets, crowds of admirers were occasionally punctuated by comedians and philosophers, daring to mock him to his face. In the Senate, the stubborn Thrasea Paetus even stormed out during a vote of thanks giving for the death of Agrippina. Across the capital, informers reported anyone who dared to suggest Nero murdered his mother without cause, but Nero refused to allow such cases to be brought to court. Perhaps he thought reacting severely would only add weight to the accusations. Or perhaps he was just riddled with guilt. Finally, he was a free man, but at what cost?

Chapter 6: A Star is Born

The Greek tale of Orestes was one of the ancient world's best-known dramas. The story begins with the Mycenae king, Agamemnon returning home from Troy, only to be slaughtered by his wife Clytemnestra and her lover. When Orestes, the son of the late king and his treacherous wife, reaches manhood, the oracle at Delphi tells him he must avenge his father's death. Orestes returns home to Mycenae in disguise and slays his mother's lover. Recognising him as her son, Clytemnestra begs him to show mercy, baring the bosom that nourished him. However, Orestes completes his duty, killing her too. Thereafter, Orestes is haunted incessantly by the goddesses of vengeance, known as the Furies. After once again consulting with the oracle at Delphi, he flees to Athens, where he is acquitted in a great trial, defended by Apollo, and winning by just one vote.

The parallel between Nero and Orestes was not lost on the Roman public. One piece of graffiti, scrawled beneath one of the emperor's statues, bluntly read: "Nero Orestes Alcmaeon, mother-slayer. Or, put it another way: Nero killed his own mother." In private, Nero complained to his inner circle that he was haunted by the ghost of his mother and expressed a terrible paranoia of the wrath of the Furies. However, the theme of the story of Orestes was not so much matricide but justified matricide. Like Orestes, though riddled with guilt, Nero told himself it was his duty to murder his mother.

Orestes's mother had killed his father, stolen his inheritance and placed the Mycenaeans beneath the tyranny of a woman. Agrippina had also sought to take power into her own hands, supporting rival claimants and allegedly even plotting to kill her own son. Nero assured himself that she had to die to preserve the safety of the empire itself. Gripped by deep remorse, he increasingly indulged himself in blurring the lines between his own life and his favourite Greek myths. His grief sparked a renewed passion for drama, which he hurled himself into with renewed vigour.

This was a serious turning point. Nero was a free man. Not only was he finally freed from the shadow of his mother, but those of his advisors too. In refusing to help Nero kill his mother, they had failed him in his hour of greatest need. With the political counterweight of Agrippina gone, they had less sway over the emperor than ever. Between his mother's interference in his love life, and Seneca's incessant orations on clemency and keeping up appearances, Nero was fed up with everyone's nagging. No longer would he abide Seneca's insistence on mitigating his basest interests. He was his own emperor now. With his darling Poppaea at his side, happy to indulge his excesses, the world was his oyster.

Soon after Agrippina's assassination, Nero's aunt Domitia succumbed to a painful and protracted death. When Nero had her will quashed, many connected the dots, speculating that the emperor had her killed in order to accelerate his inheritance of her grand estates in Baiae, home to some stunning fishponds, and Ravenna. Her body was scarcely cold when he proposed building a grand gymnasium on her land in Ravenna. Unlike Claudius, who had once disparaged an athletic senator as "that wonder of the wrestling floor", Nero was obsessed with sports. He hired his own troupe of court wrestlers and grappled with them incessantly, hoping to hone his skill.

To commemorate this new phase of his reign, and of course, his own salvation, Nero would stage the greatest spectacle Rome had ever seen, the Ludi Maximi. Offered for "the Eternity of the Empire", the Ludi Maximi saw men and women of senatorial and equestrian rank take part in a series of performances, held simultaneously across six different theatres.

Every day, Nero watched jealously from a balcony known as the proscenium of the state, as Rome's most esteemed figures disgraced themselves by acting out plays and duked it out as gladiators, for financial compensation. Some of the more conservative senators thumbed their noses, thinking it utterly contemptible for nobles to debase themselves to such depths of moral depravity. Augustus had banned senators from performing in such spectacles, be it chariot racing, acting or gladiatorial bouts. However, no one really paid it any attention, as evidenced by Tiberius's futile attempt to renew the ban. Some people just could not help themselves. As a renowned knight rode an elephant down a tightrope, Nero squirmed with envy. He wished he could have taken part, but he knew that was a bridge too far.

Instead, he contented himself with the role he was born

to play, the good emperor. It was in this capacity that he ironically starred in the Ludi Maximi's almighty climax; a riotous performance of Afranius's 2nd-Century BC play, 'The Fire'. Typical of his new approach, blurring the lines between reality and fiction, the stage was transformed into an enormous burning house. Audience members were told they could keep whatever they salvaged from the blazing inferno, sparking a mad dash into the flames.

Nero rounded off the event by raining down all manner of tickets on the adoring crowd, which could be traded for food, clothes, gold, silver, jewels, pearls, paintings, trained wild animals, ships and even apartment buildings or estates. Frantic revellers crawled over one another, clawing wildly in hopes of winning their very own golden ticket. As the festival drew to a close, Nero dedicated an enormous new marketplace on the Caelian Hill, celebrating his salvation, and the preservation of the empire.

It was a grand moment, and all of Rome seemed to be on a high. Yet, for Nero, watching Rome's elites live out his dream of performing on stage, it felt somewhat hollow. Knowing the capital was not ready for his theatrical debut, instead he turned to the less offensive pursuit of charioteering. Chariot racing was deemed somewhat less ignoble than the other spectacles, as it bore at least some correlation to the arguably greatest Roman virtue of them all; martial ability.

Everyone loved a good race. Spanning a 650-by-125-metre plot between the Palatine and Aventine Hills, the largest racing venue, the Circus Maximus, could hold up to 150,000 spectators. Romans from all backgrounds would flock to the Circus to watch charioteers risk their lives in thrilling breakneck races. Guests were seated according to social standing, with senators sat at the front atop comfy cushions they were allowed to bring from home, going all the way back to freedmen and slaves, perched atop wooden benches. There was special seating reserved for magistrates, religious officials, women, children, tutors, and even married people.

While all Romans were allowed to wear togas to the games, senators and knights differentiated themselves by wearing marks of their ranks. While soldiers donned decorations and priests put on ritualistic robes. The Circus Maximus was, in many ways, a microcosm of the capital itself, and a reflection of Roman social order. The excitement spilled out from the racetrack to the wooden arcades and markets beyond, overflowing with food vendors, shops, jugglers, astrologers and even prostitutes, keen to cater to the throngs of excited spectators.

Like actors and dancers, charioteers and gladiators were mostly comprised of former slaves from the Hellenised Eastern provinces. Much of Rome's nobility looked down on them not only as professional performers, but immoral, impious, sexually fluid purveyors of vice. Others still frowned upon the notion of public spectacles entirely, dismissing them as morally corrupt celebrations of venality, wasting money on events that unnecessarily incited mass gatherings.

That very year, a gladiatorial spectacle at Poppaea's hometown of Pompeii went awry, sparking a bloody brawl in the amphitheatre between local residents and visiting spectators. The event was so scandalous, it warranted a complaint being sent to the emperor himself. He delegated the matter to the Senate, who banned the settlement from holding games for a decade and exiled the ex-senator who organised the show.

And yet, despite their controversial conduct, Rome's most accomplished gladiators and charioteers were paradoxically celebrated across the capital as sex symbols, their faces draped across all manner of souvenirs and trinkets. Idolised by plebians and nobles alike, although the dangerous job understandably had an incredibly high turnover, those who survived enough fights grew into fabulously wealthy superstar celebrities. Frowning on this superficial veneration, Seneca remarked, "I could show you the youths of the bluest blood who are enslaved by dancers: there is no servitude more disgraceful than that which is voluntary."

The philosopher loathed frivolous blood sports that pitted man and beast against one another, believing they were cruel, and degraded the morals of their spectators. At his insistence, Nero toned down the violence of his own games. However, unfortunately for Seneca, his great protégé was utterly captivated by the great Roman spectacle. Showmanship ran in his blood. Not only did his father love to race chariots, his exhibitionist grandfather, who also staged pantomimes featuring Roman knights and married women, did too. Nero may have belonged to the Julio-Claudians now, but his blood was that of the Bronze Beards, and they were showmen through and through. If anything, it was his ancestral duty to surpass their exploits.

Not content to simply roar from the imperial box, known as the pulvinar, Nero entertained daydreams of becoming a great charioteer himself, and even began inviting members of the public to watch him practise. All the great kings and warriors, he pointed out, had raced horses. The poets sang their praises, and the gods were honoured by them. He had a point; Rome's original chariot races had been steeped in religious ritual, preceded with a religious procession, where the gods were called down from the Capitol to the Circus. Exasperated, Seneca and Burrus squeezed out what little influence they still had to convince the emperor to do so within the private confines of a specially built enclosure in his Vatican Gardens, in the valley across the Tiber. The plebian onlookers loved it, screaming and rejoicing as he thundered past. For Nero, it was a rush unlike any other.

As the 21-year-old emperor prepared to shave his bronze beard for the first time, he once again planned a ground-breaking celebration; the Juvenile Games. While the Ludi Maximi had been public, this was technically a private affair, but one that stretched over an entertainment complex spanning a theatre, amphitheatre and circus. Nero spared no expense, building a private theatre across the Tiber just for the occasion. The Tiber itself would serve as the beating heart of the festival, with food and drink booths and luxury stalls erected all along the grove surrounding the Naumachia of Augustus. Keen to make sure everyone had a good time, the emperor handed out huge quantities of spending money to people from all backgrounds, and even encouraged members of the nobility to go for singing and dancing lessons.

After shaving his beard and placing it tactfully into a golden ball, he sat back and soaked in the sight of noblemen and women performing Greek and Latin plays. Anybody who was deemed too old or ill to perform solo instead sang in chorus, and Nero banned everyone from wearing masks so none could hide behind anonymity. This, he said, was the people's will. As the Juvenile Games were technically a 'private' event, Nero was able to circumvent some of Rome's more rigid customs. Elderly former consuls took part, and one woman in her 80s even danced in a pantomime. Conservative senators once again retched in disgust as their male peers acted out women's parts, and noblewomen performed supposedly unseemly roles. But the best was yet to come.

As the Games reached a spectacular pinnacle and the stage cleared, the theatre fell into a quiet murmur of anticipation. They recalled the emperor's penchant for grandiosity, remembering the spectacular performance of The Fire at the Ludi Maximi. How would he top himself this time? What did he have in store? When the former consul, Gallio, strolled onto the stage, the room fell silent. To everyone's surprise, Gallio announced the emperor himself would now be taking to the stage. This was unprecedented. Suddenly, Nero burst onto the stage, dressed as a citharode, trailed by long flowing robes. Some could not contain their shock, punctuating the deathly silence with exasperated gasps. Burrus stood with the Praetorians, his foot shaking nervously, sweat clinging to his brow. He could barely contain his anxiety. The emperor was completely out of control.

By the time Nero took a seat, the room was so quiet one could hear his lyre creak as he shuffled into position. The crowd began to wonder, was this an elaborate joke? Suddenly, a husky voice soared over the room, crackling at first, but persevering, and finding some semblance of balance. Eyes widened and jaws dropped, as Nero crooned his way through a piece called 'Attis, or the Bacchantes'. Though the emperor was clearly a committed musician, with great proficiency on the lyre, Burrus could not help but cringe in pain. Surrounded on either side by his soldiers, he could feel the weight of the empire crushing down upon his shoulders. For a moment, he wished the world would just swallow him whole. This was humiliating.

Nero's sycophantic vocal coaches stood on the side of the stage, smiling, gesturing, and nodding. As the song dragged on, the crowd was sharply divided; some were overjoyed at their great emperor's remarkable talent, others disgusted at the obscene display. This, they thought, was a stunt worthy of that impious wretch, Caligula.

When it was over, under great duress, poor Burrus was compelled to lead the Praetorians in applause, with tears of shame in his eyes. While the crowd negotiated over how to dignify the performance, the theatre filled with an almighty roar, as a huge troupe of young soldiers applauded and yelled, "Beautiful Caesar, Apollo, Augustus, another Pythian! By yourself, we swear, Caesar, no one conquers you!" This small army was an entirely new force, of Nero's own design. It brought together the standard concept of the bodyguard with that of the Augustian youth organisation, adapted to celebrate not military exercises but Nero's artistic proficiency. Named the Augustiani, the troop was tasked with following the emperor and singing his praises; all day, every day. It was fairly typical for performers to have their own claques of supporters, but this was a farcical level of self-aggrandisement.

As it transpired, the Juvenile Games were not so much a celebration of Nero's safety, but his newfound independence. The introduction of the Augustiani, comparing Nero to Apollo was a propaganda milestone, signalling a new phase in the development of his cult of personality. Both Seneca and the ever-enthusiastic poet Calpurnius Siculus had compared Nero's singing and lyre playing to Apollo not long after his accession, and it seemed he had taken it to heart. This was a hell of a start, but if he was to ever realise his great dream of officially performing in 'public', he would have to reform upper class culture, and chip away at its more conservative views.

To Nero, intertwining his own cult of personality with the mythology of Apollo seemed like a perfect solution. Everyone revered Apollo. Apollo was not just the god of music and poetry, but of plague, archery, and prophecy too. His statues were scattered across the capital's temples, equipped with his bow and lyre, messy golden hair and a wreath, or branch of Delphic laurel, atop. His oracle, the oracle at Delphi, was the most renowned in the world, and to Homer, he represented the apex of physical and spiritual development. Most importantly, however, was his identification with Sol; the sun god, the golden charioteer, the giver of light and life, the objective judge who observes all deeds, good and bad. If music was sacred to Apollo, who, Nero asked, were the Romans to hold it in disdain?

It was Apollo whose likeness Rome's citharodes mimicked, and soon, Nero too would come to embody his divine patron, wearing his style of elevated cothurni boots and free-flowing chiton. However, this personal transformation was about more than just music. Nero's transformation into Apollo represented his own personal metamorphosis as emperor; emerging from the shadows of his mother and advisors to become a great beacon of light at the very heart of the empire.

After Nero's performance, the crowd poured out of the theatre, ecstatic and ready to celebrate the start of a new era. They boarded rafts and sailed down the Tiber, feasting and drinking through the night, courtesy of their generous emperor. After the tyranny of Tiberius, the madness of Caligula and the corruption of Claudius, finally it seemed the gods had returned to Rome. In Nero, the Romans had their very own Apollo, a brilliant bronze sun rising over a new Golden Age.

Chapter 7: Trouble in Paradise

In the summer of 60, Nero kicked his propaganda campaign into overdrive, with yet another epic spectacle. But for all the hyperbole of his earlier shows, this was a truly revolutionary act; the spark with which he would light the capital's passion for his beloved Hellenic culture. This was truly something the likes of which Romans had never seen before, Neronia: The Neronian Games. The emperor was bringing the great Greek games to Rome.

Held in August, the event would feature musical, gymnastic and equestrian competitions, modelled in strict accordance with ancient Greek tradition. While Nero encouraged nobles to take part, once again he declined to perform himself and, much to the mild disappointment of the plebians, even barred professional pantomime dancers from participating. The emperor left nothing to chance; making sure that there would be no room for riotous factional fights, lest anyone leave with a bad taste in their mouths. Keen to show he was not simply prostrating himself before Greek culture, instead of the usual two-to-four-year intervals between Greek games, Nero announced that his festival would be a quinquennial one, held every five years. Moreover, contrary to Greek custom, he named the games after himself.

For the spectacle-obsessed Romans, it was quite the show. Many had never been to Greece, let alone attended any of the great games, and would never have the opportunity to. Thrilled by the novelty of the new festival, revellers dressed up in Greek attire and flocked to the event. In a fitting appropriation, just as the Greeks used to invite the priestesses of Ceres to observe the Olympics, Nero invited the Vestal Virgins to watch the Neronian gymnastic competition.

Of course, for the emperor, the stage that mattered most was the theatre. There, Rome was introduced to the poet Lucan, a promising young talent who had travelled to Athens, only to be recalled by Nero, and handed a quaestorship well before the required legal age. Asides from both writing poetry, Nero and Lucan shared a tutor; Lucan's brilliant uncle Seneca. Lucan recited a verse eulogy he had written just for the occasion, Praise of Nero, which was so spectacularly composed, he was awarded a crown in the Theatre of Pompey.

The competitors for the Latin oratory and poetry crown, meanwhile, forfeited the title in favour of the literary emperor himself, who had watched from the orchestra, alongside the senators. It was said that the ex-consuls who judged the music competition didn't even bother holding a contest before offering Nero the crown for his lyre playing. The emperor politely declined, insisting it be carried instead to the statue of Augustus. Of course, he was quite happy to lead the procession, dressed in full citharode garb, as he laid it down at Augustus's feet.

As far as whetting Rome's appetite for Hellenic culture, the Neronia proved a roaring success, and a landmark on the road to Nero's own professional performing career. He followed up the propaganda victory with another in 61, when he dedicated a magnificent new Greek-style bath and gymnasium complex; the first of its kind in the capital. He marked the event by handing out oil to the senators and equestrians, encouraging them to embrace athletics.

Baths were one of the great pleasures an emperor could offer his people; and Nero's were no exception. Guests poured into the facility, leaving their clothes with a slave and going for a hearty workout in the attached palaestra or gymnasium. Then, they'd have their bodies oiled up and spend time in the 'frigidarium', plunging themselves into cold water, before taking a dip in the tepidarium. Although, for most, the highlight of the trip was the caldarium steam room, where guests basked in the hot plunge bath, heated by fiery furnaces. After this, servants would scrape the oil from their bodies using a tool called a strigil, sending them on their way home.

Although Nero was passionate about sharing his love of the baths with the nobles, he did not entirely lose himself to his most base desires. The emperor continued to pair his cultural reforms with practical ones, abandoning the conservative senatorial tradition of only allowing men from consular families to become consuls. Under his rule, Caesennius Paetus became the first man of non-consular descent to hold an ordinary consulship, a move that pleased many an aspiring senator.

He was also consulted on a bizarre case, where the urban Prefect, Pedanius Secundus, was murdered by one of his slaves. Four years earlier, the Senate had decreed that when a master was killed by a slave, their entire household should be tortured and put to death. At the time of his death, Pedanius had 400 slaves in his employment, so the trial caused quite a stir. Nero left the matter to the Senate to deal with, in order to appease their sense of autonomy, and distance himself from the inevitable fallout.

Much of Rome's populace were former slaves, who would have sympathised tremendously with the hundreds of innocents wrapped up in this mess. After an impassioned speech by Cassius Longinus, the Senate decided to execute all 400 slaves, in accordance with tradition. It was not a popular move. Plebs and freedmen took to the streets to demand the release of the innocent slaves, with compassionate senators standing alongside them. Armed with stones and torches, the mob clogged up the city, physically preventing the sentence from being carried out. As the situation teetered towards a riot, Nero was forced to send in the troops to break open a path to the execution site. After the mass execution, some overzealous senators suggested that Pedanius's freedmen should be banished from Italy, but Nero intervened, declaring that they should not be punished in excess of the law.

The emperor responded somewhat more graciously to a two-pronged food crisis, triggered when a storm destroyed 200 corn ships in Ostia, and a fire burned down 100 more along the Tiber. Eager to avoid mass panic, Nero dumped huge batches of spoiled corn into the river as a show of confidence, while simultaneously granting subsidies to corn dealers, out of his own pocket, to keep the market price low.

He was also deeply mired in an increasingly complex set

of foreign policies. Although Corbulo had done a tremendous job in Armenia, Rome's incompetent Armenian puppet king, Tigranes, provoked a Persian invasion by invading the neighbouring territory of Adiabene, sparking yet another diplomatic crisis. As Rome and Parthia played tug of war over Armenia, elsewhere Nero's armies established a military occupation over the Bosporous Kingdom on the northern Black Sea and annexed the kingdom of Pontus on the southern coast. The region gave Rome a crucial new supply of corn, providing much needed food security, and a strategic staging post for Rome's ongoing conflict with Parthia.

Meanwhile, in the distant northwest, the emperor continued to pacify the province of Britannia, inherited from his stepfather's invasion in 43AD. There, Nero's generals had made significant progress against the Welsh tribes, and destroyed the Druids' grip on Anglesey, denying rebels a safe haven. The Celtic Iceni king Prasutagus had even offered a powerful gesture, naming Nero and his daughters as joint heirs to his fortunes. He hoped the move would afford some protection to his family, and at least part of their rightful inheritance. He was wrong.

Rome's aristocracy saw Britannia as a huge potential cash cow. The island was an untapped market, and the Britons were desperate to acquire the latest technology and luxuries from Rome. However, they lacked the capital. Sensing an opportunity, prominent Romans, such as Seneca, loaned out copious amounts of money to the empire's new subjects, only to suddenly call in all their repayments at once. With the Britons unable to pay their debts in full, the rapacious procurator Catus Decianus resorted to predatory measures.

In the ensuing carnage, Prasutagus's house was ransacked, his wife Boudica whipped, and his daughters raped. Enraged, Boudica rose up in a great revolt, partnering with other fiercely independent tribes, such as the Trinobantes. At great cost, the general Suetonius Paullinus succeeded in putting down the rebellion, and was honoured for his efforts, but was recalled after falling out with the imperial procurator. With the province in chaos, Nero asked the prominent freedman, Polyclitus, to figure out how best to pacify the furious Britons.

Although Nero had worked tirelessly to rid his court of the corruption that had plagued Claudius's court, the sneering Polyclitus proved effective calling the Roman army in Britannia to heel. The Britons, however, found the level of power the former slave wielded ridiculous. Finally, Nero appointed the diplomatic-minded governor, Petronius Turpilianus, to focus on strengthening Rome's influence in Britannia, rather than expanding it, bringing some much-needed stability to the province.

Back in the capital, as Nero basked in his bread, games and newfound autonomy, an accusation was levelled that would soon spark off a serious political crisis. The incident began at a party, ironically held by the son of a former governor of Britannia. One of the guests, Cossutianus Capito, accused the praetor Antistius Sosinus, of reciting poetry insulting the emperor, characterising the event as an act of grave treason.

With even the host himself unable to corroborate the claim, it was clear the case should have been thrown out. Up until now, Nero had consistently upheld his inaugural vow to end all of the closed-door maiestas treason trials that had brought Claudius's reign into such disrepute. Yet, for some reason, although all of Nero's previous consuls had dismissed every single maiestas trial to date, when it came to Antistius, they did not. After eight years of clemency, Nero was going back on his word.

Although the accusation was rather farcical, the consul-designate suggested an incredibly severe punishment; reviving the ancient method of having Antistius scourged to death. Shocked, the senator Thrasea Paetus, a leading member of the so-called Stoic Opposition, who had earlier walked out of the vote of thanks for Agrippina's death, renounced the cruel sentence. Instead, he suggested Antistius be banished, and his property confiscated. With the Senate divided, the consuls referred to matter to Nero himself to decide.

The more wary senators began to suspect that Nero had conjured the entire crisis himself, as a cynical exercise in propaganda. It seemed the emperor's plan was to arrange for the Senate to suggest an absurdly harsh sentence, and then use his imperial veto to overrule it; as a way of projecting his magnanimous devotion to clemency. However, Nero had not banked on Thrasea kicking up such a stink and beating him to the punch. Thrasea's suggestion completely undermined the entire scheme.

Nero's mealy-mouthed response was to state that while Antistius deserved the harsher punishment, if the Senate had condemned him to this 'fair' sentence, he would have personally moderated its severity, out of kindness. With this in mind, he said that the Senate was free to acquit the accused if they wished, and he would not intervene. Although the incident did somewhat communicate a form of clemency or humility, it indicated a far more sinister turn in policy. It also transformed the increasingly troublesome Thrasea into a senatorial sensation. He had made no secret of his disgust over Nero's matricide and remained determined to hold power to account.

Since the time of Augustus, the empire was effectively split between imperial and senatorial authority. While Nero directly governed the military holdings in more unstable regions through legati or procurators, the rest were administrated by Senate-appointed praetors and proconsuls. These provincial assemblies had the power to decree a vote of thanks for their governors, which would be carried to Rome and announced in the Senate. Receiving one of these votes of thanks indicated an endorsement of the governor's rule and failing to secure one could mean the end of one's career. So, when Crete's wealthy oligarch Claudius Timarchus bragged that he was so powerful that he alone held the authority to determine who should receive the province's thanks, the Senate was rightly furious. If this claim were true, the entire province of Crete was corrupt, and if that was true, the entire political system was corruptible.

Determined to make an example of the narcissistic aristocrat, the Senate put him on trial, which provided Thrasea with a platform to make one of his fieriest speeches yet. Seizing the moment, he went above and beyond, denouncing not just the contemptible defendant, but the entire practice of decreeing thanks. He roared, "If such practices are stopped, our provinces will be ruled more equitably and more steadily. For as the dread of a charge of extortion has been a check to rapacity, so, by prohibiting the vote of thanks, will the pursuit of popularity be restrained."

Although the Senate gave Thrasea's suggestion an almighty ovation, it had to be sent to Nero for approval. Of course, the emperor approved, putting his name to a move that would stamp out corruption, and reinforce the authority of provincial governors. However, this time, Thrasea shared in the glory.

Not to be outdone, when one of the emperor's intimates, Fabricius Veiento was accused of using his influence to sell offices, Nero had him banished, and all of his books burned. Veiento's works became notorious collectibles, and some believed Nero simply used the opportunity to seize his property for himself. It seemed the more confident he grew in his imperial authority, the more his personal insecurities seeped through the cracks.

Nero's courtiers knew well he was a man of many talents. He had long loved writing his own poetry, especially Alexandrian satire and lyric poetry, which he personally recited in public and in private. The emperor hosted regular workshops with Rome's finest poets over dinner and was even accused of plagiarising lines from up-and-coming bards, who could scarcely protest. Whether there was any truth to this, he was clearly deeply committed to the craft, penning cheeky verses such as 'The One-Eyed Man', teasing the ex-praetor Claudius Pollio, as well as another verse mocking King Mithridates, and some, of course, celebrating his beloved chariot racing.

His work was supposedly so well received that one recitation was celebrated with a supplication to the gods, and some were written in gold, and dedicated to the Jupiter Capitolinus. Yet, for all the acclaim, he was no match for his mentor Seneca's own light verse and tragic compositions. To the emperor's consternation, it seemed that his tutor's own output seemed to grow with his own, as if he were rubbing it in.

The brilliance of Seneca's other protégé, Lucan, also exasperated Nero. Lucan's magnificent Civil War epic Bellum Civile especially infuriated him, despite opening with a shameless flattery of the jealous emperor, mirroring Virgil's praise of Augustus in the Georgics. Grotesque in excess, Lucan's invocation asserted that after death, Nero would rise to become chief of the gods, guiding the flaming chariot of Phoebus, so that the earth should never again fear the wavering sun. Lamenting the Civil Wars, he decried, "Yet if the fates could find no other way for Nero's coming, nor the gods with ease gain thrones in heaven; and if the Thunderer prevailed not till the giants' war was done, we plain no more, ye gods!"

Nero was so bitter that during one particularly masterful recitation of the book, he actively sabotaged Lucan's performance; rudely interrupting it to call an emergency meeting of the Senate. Like his uncle, Lucan believed that the while Republican system was preferable, the complex nature of the empire required the principate to maintain stability, peace, and order. However, as Nero grew increasingly hostile, laying insult upon insult, he began to respond in kind, tinging his work with pro-Republican and anti-imperial sentiment. Well aware of his gifts, Lucan was not one to hide behind humility, and his propensity to pomposity and self-advertisement only served to further enrage the emperor. After completing his questorship, his relationship with Nero completely nosedived.

He was not alone in incurring the emperor's wrath. Seneca too found himself increasingly alienated from the centre of power. He was wise enough to see that the fault lines had begun to shatter, and his influence all but disintegrated. Seneca's great vision of Nero's reign was drifting further with each passing day, as the emperor perverted it with matricide, overreach, grotesque self-indulgence and petty acts of vengeance.

Since Nero's rise to power, Seneca had tried to divert the emperor's insatiable desire for popularity into policies of clemency. Rather than simply appealing to the masses, he encouraged Nero to build general popularity across all social groups. However, Nero's discipline, and his ability to tolerate the upper classes, was dissolving by the day. Ironically, as passionate as he was for theatre, he was unable to act out that quintessential role carved out by Augustus, the reluctant dictator.

Now that he too was the target of Nero's jealousy, Seneca saw the writing on the wall, and wanted to take himself out of the emperor's sights. When his old ally, Burrus, suddenly dropped dead in 62, Seneca knew all hope for his great project was lost. Compromise had never sat well with him, and he was an idealist, ill-suited to the pursuit of power. The emperor's increasingly hostile treatment of his old teacher grew so severe, Seneca finally requested a withdrawal from public life, offering to surrender his fortunes and retire as a friend of the emperor. Nero refused.

With Burrus dead, Nero wanted to avoid his mother's mistake of concentrating so much power in the hands of one man, and once again split the responsibilities between two Praetorian Prefects. One of his new appointees was Faenius Rufus, an old ally of Agrippina who had excelled as the man in charge of the corn supply. The second Prefect was a rather more controversial choice; Nero's friend, Ofonius Tigellinus, the father-in-law of the man who had instigated the first treason trial of Nero's reign. Tigellinus was quite unlike Burrus, and as one of Nero's favourites, would soon find another advisory partner who was quite unlike Seneca. The age of clemency was over.

Chapter 8: New Management

Unlike the equestrian pedigree of Seneca and Burrus, Tigellinus was described as "obscure in parentage and debauched in early life". During his youth, his once-wealthy family had fallen out of favour; forcing him to rely upon his good looks and natural charm alone. Using these talents, he gained access to the households of Nero's father, Gnaeus, and Marcus Vinicius, as well as their wives, Agrippina and her sister Livilla. Tigellinus grew so close to the siblings that when their brother Caligula had them exiled on charges of adultery, he named Tigellinus as one of their supposed lovers, and banished him to Greece. After a few years simply getting by, perhaps as a merchant, a windfall inheritance dramatically turned his life around.

Claudius later recalled him from exile but banned him from stepping foot anywhere near the imperial palace, lest there be any truth to Caligula's accusations. In the ensuing years, Tigellinus used his inheritance to accumulate a large portfolio of land in Apulia and Calabria, where he bred racehorses. At some point, he met Agrippina's young racing-obsessed son Nero, who was thrilled by Tigellinus's horses. As Nero's prospects grew greater, Tigellinus hitched his wagon to the young boy's chariot, fanning the flames of his passion for the circus.

At the time of Burrus's death, Tigellinus had risen to the Prefect of the Watch, in charge of the capital's fire brigade.

The timing was perfect. Nero was at a turning point in his rule and was thrilled at the prospect of replacing the stern Burrus with an advisor that would not only embrace his exhibitionism, but encourage it. While Burrus had devoted his life and service to the good of the empire, all Tigellinus cared about was advancing his own position. At all costs.

By now, Nero felt sufficiently secure in his position. The Senate was assured of his clemency and the people in awe of his generosity and showmanship. He had dedicated magnificent buildings and facilities to the people and single-handedly pioneered a new piece of cultural heritage in the Neronian Games. His spectacles were second to none and his donations to the senators, soldiers and plebians alike were generous and gracious in equal measure. As a handsome young prince with the blood of Augustus and Germanicus in his veins, the common people felt closer to him than any emperor who had ever come before. His remarkable military victories over the Parthians were commemorated that very year, with a grand triumphal arch erected in in the emperor's honour. Now, the people were gradually starting to embrace him as Apollo, the harbinger of sun and song. And he was pretty impressive behind a chariot too.

As the grandson of Germanicus, and stepson of Claudius, he had links to both the Julian and Claudian lines, and with most of his rivals killed off by Agrippina, his claim by blood was second to none. The only threats left alive were Cornelius Sulla, the husband of Claudius's daughter Antonia, and Rubellius Plautus, the Stoic great-grandson of Tiberius, who Agrippina was once accused of plotting to marry and replace Nero with. However, Sulla had already been banished to Marseilles, and Plautus similarly exiled to Asia.

Acutely aware of the paranoia Agrippina had instilled in her son, Tigellinus whispered into Nero's ear, asking what would happen if Plautus plotted a revolt in the East, with the aid of Corbulo's Syrian armies? And what, he inquired, if Sulla seduced the Rhine legions to his cause? His hands already soaked in blood; Nero didn't really want to just go around killing people he didn't need to and told Tigellinus he would sleep on the supposed threats for a while. One night, however, as the night sky lit up with a passing comet, the emperor took the sight as an ill omen, foreshadowing a change of rule, and immediately dispatched assassins to murder his rivals.

Although Sulla was caught off guard, Plautus, who was both well-connected and well-liked, was warned in advance of the attack. Regardless, he made a point of standing his ground and accepting his fate, cut down by a centurion as he prepared for his daily exercise. When the heads of his two enemies arrived in the capital, Nero rejoiced, supposedly asking himself of Plautus, "Why, Nero, did you fear a man with such a big nose?" After, he wrote to the Senate to applaud the demise of the agitators and the Senate, in turn, responded feebly; once again voting to give thanks, and expel the duo from their ranks. Nero had finally completed his mother's efforts to purge all other members of the royal bloodline. Now, he alone was the sole heir to the Julio-Claudian dynasty, the last descendent of Augustus.

Why, then, should he continue dragging out the charade of his farcical, loveless marriage to Claudius's daughter Octavia? Sure, the marriage did boost his credentials, but at what cost? Three long years had passed since Agrippina's death. Nero's passion for Poppaea was one of the driving forces behind the act, and while the murder had freed them to see one another, it was not enough; Nero needed Poppaea entirely. Now she was divorced from Otho, after years of waiting, the emperor was utterly overcome by desire for his beautiful, captivating, and sharp-minded muse.

Nero had once asked Burrus about divorcing Octavia, only for the Praefect to spit back, "Well then give her back her dowry," in reference to the throne. But Burrus was dead now, and the throne was secure. Seneca did not approve of the union either, but there was very little the austere spoilsport did approve of. Besides, Nero had plotted his mother's the murder alone, and it had gone perfectly; Romans of all backgrounds were still celebrating his salvation. What did Seneca and Burrus know?

While Octavia had failed to bear Nero a child, Poppaea had already produced a son from her first marriage. More importantly, she was pregnant with Nero's child. With a potential heir on the way, the emperor had more to gain than ever. There could be no more powerful way to seal his grip over the empire than with a biological son and heir. Unlike his predecessor, Tigellinus did little to dissuade Nero, who insulted his wife Octavia with increasing frequency and vitriol. After an alleged attempt to assassinate his spouse failed, Nero simply divorced her, declaring her barren and sterile and sending her off to Campania under armed guard. Instead of her dowry, he simply gave her the property taken from Burrus and Plautus. The princeps then rushed into marrying his beloved Poppaea, fully expecting to live happily ever after.

But the people were not happy. It soon became abundantly clear to Nero why Burrus had been so opposed to the move. He had grossly misjudged public sentiment; no matter how popular he was, Octavia was far more beloved. She was widely held up as the ideal Roman woman, the epitome of virtue. Poppaea, on the other hand, was characterised as a pompous, vainglorious, licentious social climber.

Outraged at Octavia's ill-treatment, the plebians rose up revolt, storming through narrow streets towards the Capitol. As the angry crowds amassed into a raging mob, suddenly a rumour started travelling around that Nero had seen the error of his ways. Ecstatic, the people screamed their thanks to the gods, and celebrated the impending return of Octavia by hurling over the newly erected statues of Poppaea and erecting those of Octavia in the temples and the Forum, draped in flowers. They then pushed forwards, amassing outside the imperial palace, to offer their thanks to the wise emperor himself. As the wild sea of revellers crashed against the gates, threatening to breach the walls, the hysteria drove some to attempt to break in.

Poppaea watched on impatiently as Nero shook with terror. This was an incredibly dangerous situation. Was he going to give in to their demands, and actually recall

Octavia? If he did that, she was finished. Summoning every ounce of charm, she softly appealed to her lover, warning him that Octavia's friends and slaves must have stoked the rebellion. If he folded now at this critical moment, she advised, it would set a terrifying precedent. For, if the 22-year-old Octavia were allowed to return, she would wield her influence over the mob and set them against Nero himself. Poppaea told him not to blame the plebians, the true Romans, for their insurrection, but to blame the wicked woman who had led them astray. Emboldened, Nero roared to his soldiers to disperse the crowd and let them know who was in charge. He set them loose on the mob, violently beating and bludgeoning them, and scattering them by sword point. Now he just needed an excuse.

Desperate to spin the divorce into a victory for the empire, as he had with his mother's murder, Nero had his interrogators brutally torture Octavia's maids, to procure false testimonies against her. Yet, they refused to break, such was their loyalty. They endured profound brutality, refusing to betray the virtuous Octavia, and one even spitting to Tigellinus that "Octavia's body was chaster than his own mouth".

This was a desperate situation, which called for desperate measures. Since the death of his mother, the emperor had been too overcome with guilt to meet his old pal, Anicetus. However, with Octavia's maids refusing to testify against her, and no dirt to dig up on the sweet young lady, he had no choice but to fabricate it. Once again, he summoned the admiral, and forced him to testify before a bogus council of intimates that he had committed adultery with Octavia. With that, an edict was sent out announcing that Octavia had tried to seduce the commander of the fleet of Misenum, in order to secure his loyalty, and later had an abortion. For his lies, Anicetus was exiled to Sardinia, while Octavia was shipped off to the island of Pandateria, the same island Tiberius's wife Julia was once exiled to for her promiscuity.

Octavia spent the next few days locked up in grim squalor, surrounded by cold, blank-faced centurions, her mind racing over what fate lay in store for her. She begged to know what was to become of her, only to be hit by a wall of indifference, constantly closing in on her. Such callous surroundings ill-befitted so virtuous a woman, and the delay in sentencing was perhaps a deliberate act of psychological torture, prolonging her suffering with lingering terror.

When the executioners stepped into her room, eyes burning with emotionless violence, she knew the order had come. She pleaded quietly for her life, in the name of the Germanici, the family to which she and the emperor belonged. Silence. Panicking, she implored in the accursed name of Agrippina, but again fell on deaf ears. The hardy men did not even offer her the opportunity to die on her own terms. Instead, they designed a butchery most vile, binding her up so tightly she couldn't move, before slowly carving open her veins one-by-one. Adding psychological to physical torture, Octavia knew their method was designed to give the impression that she had inflicted the wounds herself. However, as she bled and screamed, the agonising death began dragging on too long. Impatient, the men hauled her off and dunked her into a scorching hot vapour bath, where she boiled and suffocated to death, a burned and bloody mess.

Later, her killers cut off her head and shipped it back to Rome, for Poppaea to gloat over. In the aftermath, Nero had the servile Senate not only condone the treatment of Octavia but give thanks yet again. Nero and Poppaea tied up their loose ends by poisoning the once-powerful freedmen Doryphorus, who had opposed their marriage, and Pallas; Messalina's spectacularly wealthy old ally who had thought himself a magistrate. Nero had once again tempted fate, bet it all and seemingly emerged unscathed. However, while the people had little choice but to accept what had happened, this time it left a bitter taste in many a Roman heart. Octavia's admirers would softly remark that her wedding day had been her funeral.

Poppaea took to her new role as the most powerful lady in Rome with uncanny ease. As Seneca's influence continued to wane, she and Tigellinus emerged as Nero's two most powerful advisors. When a dispute broke out between Rome's client king of Judea, Herod Agrippina II, and some of his local Jewish priests, Poppaea sensed an opportunity to test out her newfound clout. Agrippa resided in the Hasmonaean palace, 200 yards west of the Temple of Jerusalem, and enjoyed watching the priests scurry through the Temple as he dined. So much so that he built a dining room specifically overlooking the Temple. The priests, however, did not appreciate being spied on in this manner, and erected a wall on the western side of the inner court to block Agrippa's view. This had the added effect of obscuring Agrippa's view of the western colonnade, where Roman soldiers mounted guard during festivals.

Agrippa raised the issue with Rome's procurator, Porcius Festus, who agreed, and ordered the priests to tear the wall down. However, the priests refused, arguing that they could not possibly demolish any part of the sacred Temple, and asked Festus to refer the matter to the emperor. Eager to avoid a diplomatic crisis, the procurator agreed, sending a dozen envoys, including the high priest and Temple treasurer to Rome. Poppaea had a great interest in the Jewish faith, and was seen as sympathetic to the oppressed minority group. Moved by the Jews' plight, she intervened on their behalf, convincing her husband to rule in their favour. The wall would stay.

On another occasion, Poppaea assisted the Jewish chronicler Josephus in securing the release of some priests who had been sent to Nero in chains on a trivial charge. When the post of procurator of Judea came up for grabs, she had her friend's husband Gessius Florus appointed to the post. Gessius and his wife both hailed from Greek cities, with underlying antisemitic tendencies, and his appointment would later prove to be incredibly ill-advised.

However, nothing highlighted Poppaea's heightened status so much as giving birth to Nero's first child, their daughter Claudia. Born on January 21, 63, in Nero's own birthplace of Antium, Claudia so thrilled the emperor, he elevated both mother and daughter with the title Augusta. Even Poppaea's hometown of Pompeii too was raised by her rising tide and made an official colony. It was a dramatic turnaround for the settlement where just years earlier, the Senate had ordered a decade-long ban on all gladiatorial games. The emperor was absolutely overcome with joy, and he'd be damned if he'd let that accursed Stoic, Thrasea, ruin his mood. Making a point of this, when he invited the entire Senate to celebrate with him in Antium, he childishly told Thrasea he wasn't invited to the party.

Rome thanked the gods profusely for the blessing; proposing a temple be built to the fertility goddess Fecundity and decreeing public games. They even added golden statues of the two Antium goddesses of Fortune to the throne of Capitoline Jupiter in Rome, and established a chariot race in Antium, to honour the Claudian and Domitian families. However, the celebrations were short-lived. Just four months later, the young Claudia died suddenly, sending Nero into a tailspin. The emperor, already an unstable, wildly emotional man, was beside himself with grief. Consumed by heartbreak, he elevated his darling daughter to the Goddess Claudia, with her own temple and priest. It was little conciliation for the chasm that had ruptured within his heart.

Nero began the long road to recovery the only way he knew how; throwing public spectacles. He embraced the great escape of Rome's many escapes with greater vigour than ever before. In the process, his obsession with theatre began to transcend itself, blurring the lines between art and life in an increasingly alarming manner. He toured Rome's great venues, such as the Amphitheatre of Statilius in the

Campus Martius, a massive looming, open cylinder of death, where spectators basked in the blood of gladiators, beasts and criminals alike.

The Campus Martius was also home not just to the 12,000-seater Theatre of Pompey, but the 13,000-person Theatre of Marcellus and the 8,000-seater Theater of Balbus too. Of the many dramatic and musical performances he watched there, Nero loved the pyrrhic dances the most; realistic re-enactments of his favourite Greek myths, inspired by the old Greek war dances. On one occasion, during an exceptionally realistic rendition of the Fall of Icarus, the poor performer playing Icarus fell from a great height, crashing to the ground so violently, his blood splattered across the emperor's face. The boundaries of performance were very fluid, and just as gladiators infused their own real-life performances with theatre, actors might engage in real sex and violence on stage. This was the nature of the great Roman spectacle. As he watched on, drifting deeper into fantasy, Nero continued to plot his own route to the stage.

Knowing that the most resistance to his performing career would come from the nobility, he continued to make them complicit, indulging their own lust for attention. Nobles and knights leapt at the chance to take to the stage or fight in the arena. In a further act of reform, the emperor abolished the safety trench that wrapped around the Circus Maximum, protecting spectators from the action beyond, in order to build a brand-new row of seats, reserved for knights from the equestrian order. The moves coincided with Nero's evolution as a performer. Soon, all the world would fawn at the feet of his god-like talents. It was only a matter of time.

Chapter 9: Hidden Music

Nero's closest confidantes had grown accustomed to his favourite mantra, the Greek proverb, "Hidden music wins no respect". Having mastered the lyre, swept up by the delirium of grief, he was desperate to share his talents with the empire, and make official his rebirth as Apollo. After the first Neronia, lyre contests made a habit of simply sending their crowns straight to the emperor, as the only man worthy of victory, even if he did not perform. When envoys came to him bearing crowns, he received them with glee, wining and dining them, and when some of the Greeks among them asked for a private performance, he proclaimed, "Only the Greeks know how to listen, and only they are worthy of my efforts!"

In 64, he finally decided on the perfect spot for his official public musical debut; the city of Naples. Of all the Bay of Naples's pleasure resorts, its namesake was regarded as the most truly Hellenised city on the Italian Peninsula. When powerful Romans needed some downtime, they flocked there in Greek robes to lay back in a bed of Greek culture. The city was home to Italy's only quinquennial Greek games, the Italica Romaea Sebasta Olympia; held in as high regard as Greece's own four ancient festivals. Nero knew that unlike the conservative, stuffy Romans, the Napolitano audience were sure to appreciate his great gift.

Accompanied by a cohort of Roman elites, as Nero took

to the stage, he addressed his adoring audience in Greek, revelling in the moment. By now he was absolutely drowning in dopamine, and a hearty dose of adrenaline. Although struck with stage fright, the sight of thousands of adoring fans was enough to loosen up his fingers and throat. Besides, he'd already had the theatre gates shut and locked, so no one could leave, even if they wanted to. It's not like he needed to fight for their attention; this was an unprecedented moment.

Suddenly, the emperor steadied himself, and adopted a stern composure. He readied his heart and mind, replaying years of practice, feeling the callouses between his fingers, recalling the heavy lead weights upon his chest. He recalled all the adversity he had overcome to reach this point, the disparaging remarks of his mother and Seneca, the fury of being confined to the prison of the royal box. As the room fell silent, he exhaled, paused, and began plucking his lyre. The crowd looked on in awe as their emperor crooned passionately through a bevy of beautiful tunes.

Watching from the shadows, Seneca could do little but cringe in disgust; perhaps, for a moment, wishing he could swap places with his dear Burrus, sure to be turning in his grave. When Nero finally finished his performance, as his Augustiani whooped and beat their hands together furiously, a group of Alexandrian visitors broke out in wild rhythmic applause, utterly thrilling the emperor. Henceforth, the Augustiani would be taught to clap in this manner, divided into small groups, each perfecting a different set of elaborate claps, or 'buzzings', with names such as 'the Tiles' and 'the Bricks'.

As the ovation reached a thunderous climax, suddenly the ground itself began to shake and grumble, rocking the theatre. With the walls and ceiling threatening to implode, chaos broke out, sending the crowd screaming and scrambling over one another for the exits. Nero's performance had triggered an earthquake, so powerful it brought the theatre crashing down on itself. When the aftershocks died down, some of the exasperated nobles felt a dagger of dread pierce their guts; this was an awful omen. Nero's disgraceful performance had enraged the gods. Others rejoiced; the fact that no one was hurt in the disaster was a miracle. Apollo had arrived.

Nero himself wrote a poem thanking the gods for protecting the audience. Buoyed by his wonderful reception, the emperor stayed in the city for days, bathing in the town, dining publicly in the orchestra, talking in Greek with random strangers and promising to sing another number once he had a few more drinks down him.

Nero was on a high. The enthusiastic response he received at Napoli convinced him to take his show on the road, with a tour of Achaia, in Greece, where the people were sure to appreciate his art. The princeps journeyed as far inland as Beneventum, where he planned to travel over the Appian Way to the port of Brundisium, on the eastern shore of the Italian Peninsula. As he watched a riotous local gladiator show, organised by one of his lackeys, Nero daydreamed of sailing over the Adriatic Sea to Greece, and perhaps even competing in the great festivals. However, that evening, his grand tour was cut short by some shocking news; in the emperor's absence, his second cousin Decimus Iunius Silanus Torquatus had been charged with attempted revolution and committed suicide. It was time to head back to Rome.

No sooner had Nero returned, in yet another U-turn, he announced he would be going on a great adventure to the East. He was particularly giddy about visiting Alexandria, where the Prefect of Egypt had constructed a special set of baths just for the occasion. Puffing out his chest, the emperor even boasted that he would join mighty Corbulo on his campaign against the Parthians. To reassure his adoring subjects, he issued an edict letting them know that he would not be gone long, and that the state would prosper in his absence. For good measure, he embarked on a rushed farewell tour of the city's temples to sacrifice to the gods, for a safe return.

After a quick stop at the Capitol, he made his way to the Temple of Vesta, on the Forum's east side, and knelt down in prayer. As he stood back up, his robe became caught on something, and he was suddenly struck blind, as his body began convulsing and trembling all over. When he awoke from the fit, in a cold sweat, he immediately perceived the event as an ill-omen. Once again, declaring his love for his homeland, he called the whole trip off, insisting that the gods wanted him to stay in Rome to protect it from harm.

He even propagandised the incident, minting new coins celebrating his commitment to the capital; adorned with images of the great market he dedicated years earlier. This new coinage was a radical departure from tradition; for the first time in his reign, the mint issued large quantities of token coinage in the full range of denominations; the sestertii, dupondii, asses, semisses and quadrantes.

Until now, larger coins, such as the sestertii and dupondii, had been minted in brass, or a copper and zinc alloy called orichalcum, and had drastically declined in colour and appearances. Nero's new brass coins were a striking golden-yellow, and he even used this beautiful colour for smaller denominations, rather than just sticking with copper. Pairing Greek technical skill with Roman aesthetic realism, the new range marked the artistic peak of Roman coinage. Larger coins depicted ultra-realistic images of the emperor, growing increasingly bloated, with hints of idealisation; his head tilted upright and his eyes deep set, in the Greek style. The coins also propagandised Nero's cult of Apollo, depicting him with thick, flowing hair, falling down in "steps" or curls; mirroring the locks of Apollo the Citharode. Although Nero kept a clean shave, the coins gave him a beard, perhaps in recognition of his biological Bronze Beard legacy.

While Napoli had loved his musical public debut, Nero knew the capital simply wasn't ready for a singing emperor. But the fire had been lit; there was no going back now, the emperor must perform. So, instead, he enjoyed another first; his first chariot race. It was perfectly in keeping with his rebrand, Apollo was not just the god of song, but the charioteer of the sun.

That summer, he held another of his grand spectacles, where the stage was repeatedly flooded and drained for a series of shows, including a wild beast hunt, mock sea-battle and gladiatorial bouts. Later, the snivelling

Tigellinus organised a bloated, debauched banquet, hosted atop a gigantic raft, built just for the occasion, on the Lake of Marcus Agrippa, near the Campus Martius. The raft was fashioned from countless wooden planks, fixed atop empty wine flasks, with soft bedding and purple carpets draped atop. It was towed by smaller boats, decked with gold and ivory trimmings, and manned by troupes of male prostitutes, ranked by age. On either side of the lake exotic birds and animals, wandering about along either side of the quays, alongside taverns and brothels staffed by noblewomen.

The 'banquet' rapidly descended into an unfettered orgy of decadence and depravity, running for several days. Naked revellers stumbled about aimlessly, fornicating out in the open, and for a brief time, mirroring the Saturnalia festival, all rules went out of the window. Slaves slept with their mistresses in front of their masters, and gladiators seduced young maidens while their fathers had sex with prostitutes in the next room.

At one point, consumed by this the spirit of hedonistic compulsion, Nero was married in a formal ceremony to one of his freedmen, the notorious pervert, Pythagoras. This time, the emperor was the bride, embracing the nuptials with all the seriousness it warranted. Not only did he wear a bridal veil, but supposedly consummated the marriage in full view of the public, with seemingly less stage fright than his performance at Napoli.

Chapter 10: Inferno

By the summer of 64, the omens were beginning to stack up. The comet, the earthquake in Napoli, Nero's fit in the Temple of Vesta. And yet, the emperor felt more assured than ever. So, on July 18, when a few shops on the crowded southeastern end of the Circus Maximus caught fire, near the Palatine and Caelian hills, at first it didn't really seem like a big deal. Riddled with notoriously narrow, claustrophobic streets and buildings made from timber, fires broke out across the capital all the time. The city's firefighter service was also hopelessly inadequate, equipped with little more than blankets and pails of water and vinegar. However, as the flames licked their way through the merchandise, the powerful summer winds rapidly bellowed them into a firestorm.

Before long, the inferno had exploded out of control, tearing 650 metres across the length of the Circus, howling through the Colosseum Valley and the Domus Transitoria; the palace Nero had hoped would connect the Palatine with the Gardens of Maecenas on the Esquiline. Soon almost all of Rome was transformed into a raging hellscape. The city's inadequate fire-fighting force was utterly overwhelmed. This was a fire like no other. It raged for six long days, tearing its way through the lower reaches of the Esquiline, before finally being slowed down by some strategically demolished buildings. However, just as Rome began to heave a sigh of relief and assess the damage, a second blaze broke out north of the Capitoline Hill, burning for yet another three painful days. By the time the flames finally subsided, Rome was in ruins. Thick plumes of smoke choked residents, as they desperately scoured the rubble of their homes for prized possessions.

As the smoke slowly lifted, the apocalyptic scale of the disaster sunk in; countless shops, apartment buildings, large private houses and temples alike lay in smouldering ruins. The temples of Vesta, Luna and Jupiter Stator had all perished, alongside some of Rome's most cherished ancient masterpieces of art, and victory trophies. Three of Rome's fourteen regions had been razed to the ground, seven more devastated, and only four remained untouched.

Nero, who was in his birthplace of Antium when the fire broke out, left the seaside resort with due haste. In Rome's great hour of need, he responded with the swiftness and seriousness it warranted. This was a catastrophe of epic proportions, one that had left 200,000 people homeless. Eager to pull the people back from the brink of despair, he not only swung open the Campus Martius and buildings of Agrippa to the homeless, but even his own private gardens. Furthermore, with food supplies devastated, he hauled in supplies from Ostia and temporarily discontinued the corn dole, releasing huge stores onto the market to keep prices low, and confidence high.

Although the emperor was determined to rebuild the city as quickly as possible, with two thirds of it in ruins, he sensed a unique opportunity to do so in his own image. Rome's great artist had the most glorious canvas of them all to work with; the capital itself. As reconstruction began, his first priority was a pragmatic one; make the city more fire-proof. He rolled out a sweeping series of regulations; reviving Augustus's long-ignored height limits, issuing rules against the use of timber and shared walls, and introducing fire-resistant stone. Streets were widened and laid out more frequently, while apartment complex congestion was reduced with the use of internal courtyards and porticoes on ground floor exteriors, which also served to protect passers-by from falling debris. To deter looting, rubble was left in place for a while, before being removed for free, and shipped down the Tiber on corn ships. Meanwhile, even the aqueducts were reformed, with a new group of supervisors appointed to protect public water supplies.

In yet another ambitious move, the emperor announced he would push the walls of Rome as far as the port of Ostia, bringing the sea from the "old city" into Rome. After the fire, Rome's insatiable need to bring supplies in from Ostia pushed the Tiber, with its winding channel and powerful currents, to its limits. Nero hoped to connect his Ostia-Rome canal with another planned new channel, running from Lake Avernus to Ostia. Claudius had first developed Ostia from a natural bay into an artificial harbour, to which Nero had put the finishing touches. However, like Claudius before him, Nero knew he would face huge opposition to an engineering project of this magnitude, which were traditionally dismissed by envious senators as impractical and hubristic symbols of tyrannical megalomania.

While Nero financed some of these works, such as the

new porticoes, out of his own pocket, the fire had consumed so many tools, valuables, supplies, properties, savings, jobs and lives, that he could scarcely burden the cost alone. His plans to spread residences out over greater areas would create a housing shortage, which could only be met by dramatically expanding the city itself. Most of the reconstruction effort was privatised; with cleared areas handed back to building owners, and rewards offered to anyone who could build houses or apartment blocks within a set period of time. Hoping to incentivise private initiative, the emperor relieved provincial importers from various harbour dues and their ships from property tax.

When the imperial treasury was exhausted, Nero turned to the neighbouring provinces, demanding so much from them, many were left bankrupt. Meanwhile, his procurators pillaged temples across Rome, Asia and Achaia, looting whatever valuables they could, including statues of the gods and even gifts. Gold, silver, and bronze coinage, which had just enjoyed a renaissance, were permanently devalued; with brass and copper reintroduced for larger, and smaller denominations, respectively.

As Rome mobilised into full gear, Nero's vision began taking shape. At the heart of his new city would be a magnificent new palace, an architectural marvel worthy of the almighty Roman capital. He called it the Domus Aurea, the Golden House, a physical manifestation of the dawn of Rome's new golden age, heralded under the wise leadership of Nero Apollo. It was a microcosm of his own role as the great sun burning bright at the centre of the solar system of empire. While his previous works, the amphitheatre, market, and bath-gymnasium, had been ambitious in scale and detail, this was something else entirely, relentlessly uncompromising. Spanning half the city, it would span a network of residential buildings, punctuated by forests, pastures, vineyards, fields, long vistas, clearings, animals, fountains, and central artificial lake.

The palace grounds sprawled across the slopes of the Esquiline in the north, the Caelian to the south and the Palatine to the west, stretching between approximately 125 and 200 acres. The main residential complex' façade devoured the Oppian Hill, on the Esquiline, where terraces were carved into the landscape, and parts of the hill behind terraformed, to create a clear east-west orientation. Facing south, the 360-metre-long façade would glisten in the sun all day, creating a dazzlingly blinding effect of grandiosity.

The double-story palace featured a five-sided trapezoidal court in the west wing, mirrored by another on the east wing, with a domed octagonal room in the centre, radiating out symmetrically into five rooms. Its most magnificent feature was a spellbinding revolving dining room, with a fretted ceiling of ivory, which showered perfume and flowers movable panels and pipes. Perhaps powered by water running through a device suspended through the dome's opening, as it rotated, the room seemed to represent world revolving around the sun, Nero himself. The interiors were just as magnificent as the architecture; with the master painter Famulus spending all day straddling scaffolding, painting in expensive pigments of red, blue, gold, and purple. These masterpieces included garden imagery, seeming to enlarge rooms, and interpretive mythical scenes, drawing observers into interacting with the building itself.

Nearby, Nero even rebuilt the Temple of Fortuna, which was said to house a statue rescued from a shrine constructed by King Servius Tulius in the 6th century BC. Composed of a newly discovered brilliant white marble with striking yellow veins, from Cappadocia, it was gilded and bejewelled all over, glistening once again like fire in the sun.

To reach the palace from the Forum, visitors would travel up the Via Sacra, which was widened, straightened and made steeper, as it climbed towards the magnificent entrance. Along either side were arcades, framed with pillared halls, adding to the sense of spectacle and depth. Atop the Velian Hill, the journey culminated in the palace entrance, marked by a herculean 120-foot bronze statue of Sol, signifying the move from the old Republican centre of Rome to the heart of the imperial empire. As work began, many feared Nero was actually building a statue of himself in the likeness of Apollo, on a scale reserved exclusively for the gods, so that it could be seen all across the capital.

During his more opulent parties, rather than depriving citizens of their city, Nero was said to have treated the whole city like his home, where every Roman was welcome. Now, however, it seemed he was taking it a little too literally. While his previous palace, the Domus Transitoria, had respected Rome's existing infrastructure, this project gobbled up all in its path. Some of the surrounding lands still belonged to private owners, and areas such as the Valley of the Colosseum were home to vast commercial zones before the fire. He even flattened the temple to Claudius that his mother had begun building on the Caelian Hill. Nero's timing could scarcely be worse. Set against a time of mass suffering, desolation and economic ruin, the project was the very physical embodiment of hubris.

This fact was not lost on anyone. One witty piece of graffiti referenced an ancient proposal to abandon the capital after the Gallic invasion of 390BCE: "All Rome is becoming a single house. Flee to Veii, citizens". Seneca himself wrote a veiled criticism of the solar ideology, and its physical manifestation as the Golden House, "People seem to think that the immortal gods cannot give any better gift than wealth, or even possess anything better…And finally, when they would praise an epoch as the best, they call it the 'Golden Age'." Disgusted with Nero's ransacking of temples and pomposity, the philosopher once again politely asked to leave the city and retire from his advisory role and was once again refused. Instead, he withdrew into his chamber, a recluse.

Nero's Golden House was considered so vast, so tone-deaf and so self-aggrandising that it sparked off a series of vicious rumours, alleging that the emperor himself had started the fire. According to the gossip, the emperor had long loathed the ugly aesthetic of the capital, and wished to raze it to rubble, to clear the way for a new city called Neropolis, in the Hellenistic fashion of self-edification, such as Alexandria. Some whispered that the second blaze broke out on Tigellinus's estates, while others claimed they had personally seen gangs of men darting about the city, setting buildings alight.

It wasn't long before the story took on a life of its own, drawing on other aspects of Nero's supposedly self-serving behaviour; most notably, his professional singing career. A dangerous rumour began to spread as quickly as the fire itself. It alleged that when Nero returned from Antium, the first thing he did was dress in an elaborate citharode's costume, climb to the roof of his palace on the Palatine, and perform a musical rendition of 'The Capture of Ilium', using the inferno as a dramatic backdrop. The story painted Nero as a treasonous, psychopathic, trivial, lunatic pyromaniac, to whom Rome's suffering was merely a prop for his theatrical flights of fancy.

Although later writers would lap this story up with glee, there was no basis for any such rumour. Not only had fire destroyed Nero's own newly constructed apartments on the Palatine and Oppian Hills, but it broke out a few days after a full moon. With the moon shining bright, it would have been impossible for the emperor to send out arsonists without being detected. Regardless, for a devastated Roman public desperate for closure, it was a good story. The rumours soon snowballed to a point where Nero could no longer afford to simply dismiss them. Rome was in mourning; they had lost their homes, their loved ones and their most prized possessions. The people were furious, grieving and desperate for answers. Nero needed to stop the flames of fury with a controlled demolition. He needed a scapegoat.

After the blaze, the emperor had taken great care to appease the gods with a series of prayer and sacrifice. During these events, a tiny sect of Jews refused to take part in the sacrifices to Vulcan and Juno. They were the followers of an obscure messianic figure called Christ, who had been crucified decades earlier in Judea, under the reign of Tiberius. Most Romans had never even heard of Jesus of Nazareth before, and his followers seemed like as a sort of Eastern Armageddon cult, an extremist offshoot of the Jewish religion, who were seen as loathing Rome's people and gods with equal fervour. Desperate to deflect the blame from himself, Nero saw the Christians as the perfect scapegoat. Keen to offer Rome some sort of catharsis to purify its grief, he arbitrarily accused them instead.

Thus began the first of many violent persecutions against the sect, as Nero rounded up every Christian he could, convicting them not of arson, but "hatred for the human race". For this supposed crime, they were sentenced to a series of disgustingly brutal and tastelessly theatrical executions. On one occasion, Nero hosted a private circus in his Vatican Gardens, where Christians were crucified and burned alive, serving as macabre mood lighting. Amidst the screams and crackles, Nero wandered about the plebs, greeting his guests, smugly dressed as charioteer. The flames upon their flesh were a symbolic form of retribution for the damage done to Rome, offering visitors an outlet for their fury. Other equally unfortunate Christians were wrapped in the skins of wild beasts and torn apart by dogs, before hysterical audiences.

These were not simply creative manners of execution but metaphorical allegories recreating violent scenes from myths, designed to exact vengeance for the most prestigious buildings lost to the fire. For extinguishing the Luna Noctiluca on the Palatine, Christians were lit alight. Those torn apart by dogs mirrored the fate of Actaeon, who was punished for watching Diana bathe. Ironically, while Nero hoped these acts would provide a bloody catharsis for the exhausted Roman public, many could not help but pity the pitiful followers of Christ.

Yet, Nero's wrath did not end with the Christians. Intensely jealous of his poetic rival, Lucan, he banned him from reciting poetry. In response, the furious Lucan launched a series of scathing satirical attacks on the emperor and his associates, even accusing him of starting the fire; to the joy of Nero's enemies. Nero may have appeased the masses, but among the nobles, the seeds of resentment were beginning to bear fruit.

Chapter 11: The Emperor Must Die

Lucan was not alone in his growing resentment towards the emperor. As much as the masses loved his performances as a charioteer and musician, they provoked more disgust among the conservative elites than he could grasp. Increasingly, it seemed that since murdering his own mother, the emperor had increasingly descended into depraved licentiousness and fickle homicidal violence. Though he had responded to the fire as well as any emperor could, much of the cost of rebuilding the capital fell on the wealthy nobility. For some, his gratuitous Golden House project was a step too far, draining some of the most powerful and prosperous provinces, for the sake of a vanity project, in the empire's greatest hour of need.

Asides from Lucan, Nero had insulted the senator Afranius Quintianus in a rude of poem of his own, mocking him as effeminate. As more slighted nobles joined a grumbling chorus of disgruntled senators and equestrians, their discontent grew into a very serious plot to bring about the emperor's downfall. By the time the consuls took office in 65, it was widely known that Poppaea was pregnant again. If she were to give birth to a son and heir, this would reinforce Nero's legitimacy, rendering any further plots against him futile.

Modelling their scheme on the assassination of Julius Caesar, the plotters were determined not to repeat the mistakes of Caligula's killers, who failed to prepare a coherent plan for what would come next. Thanks to the emperor's, and his mother's, own ruthlessness, Nero was now virtually the last of the royal bloodline. Once he was dead, to avoid the risk of civil war, the plotters would need to nominate a worthy leader, who could not just quickly fill the vacuum, but be accepted by the people, Senate and Praetorian Guard. As far as they were concerned, that man was Calpurnius Piso, a popular descendent of Republican nobility, who had inherited vast wealth from his mother, and a powerful network of contacts from his father.

Piso was tall, handsome, articulate, wrote poetry and was a master draughts player. Ironically, like the emperor, he had sung on stage in the past, but so had many nobles. He certainly hadn't made a point of it. Although the plotters knew better than to approach Tigellinus, crucially, they secured the loyalty of Faenius Rufus, the Praetorian Prefect who served alongside him. Having enjoyed the patronage, mentorship and protection of Agrippina, perhaps even her bedroom, he was still bitter about her murder.

A popular man himself, Rufus was able to rope in many of the other Praetorian officers still loyal to Agrippina; to ensure as smooth a succession for Piso as possible. After the murder, Piso would be whisked from the Temple of Ceres to the Praetorian Camp, where Faenius and his men would proclaim him emperor. This was a gamble; while Burrus had managed to keep the Guard in check after Agrippina's death, Tigellinus was now more influential among the Guard then Faenius. He had made the rest of the Guard complicit in the emperor's scandals, by coercing them into applauding the debacle in Naples. The only thing that kept the Praetorian Tribune Subrius Flavus from cutting the emperor down there and then, in full view of the entire theatre, was that it would have meant certain death for him too.

Unconvinced of Piso's suitability, Rufus added a little twist to the plot; after Nero's assassination, he would order the guard to cut down Piso himself, and instead replace him with Seneca. What good, he scowled, would it do to replace a lyre player with a tragic actor? Seneca had already been the first choice of some of the other conspirators, but even if he was aware of the plot, he refused to take part. He had long tired of betraying his scruples for the sake of public office.

Obviously, the easiest option would be to simply invite Nero to visit Piso's villa in Baiae. Once he arrived, without his guards, the men could surround, ambush and kill him at their leisure. However, Piso refused, arguing no one could respect a man who so betrayed the duty of hospitality or acted in so cowardly a manner. More importantly, the move would have left a power vacuum back in the capital.

Instead, the plotters preyed on Nero's love of the circus, and the customary openness it afforded those who wished to petition him. Enraged at the return of the freedmen, Nero's undermining of the Senate and various other offences, Plautius Lateranus volunteered to present a petition to Nero, before seizing his knees, while the rest set upon him with daggers. In preparation for the event, Lateranus announced his intent to present the petition, and when asked by Nero's secretary what the nature of the petition was, spat, "If I wish to discuss it, I will do so with your master".

With Nero distracted by the plans for his upcoming second Neronian Games, the plot quickly gathered steam; so quickly that the plotters lost control. As the date of the coup, April's Circensian Games, drew nearer, the group sent a freedwoman called Epicharis to enlist an officer from the fleet of Misenum. However, rather than joining the scheme, he immediately informed Nero, who had Epicharis arrested.

To make matters worse, the night before the attack, the loose-lipped senator Scaevinus made the fateful mistake of asking a freedman to sharpen his dagger on a whetstone "until the edge glittered". Sensing treachery was afoot, as the sun rose the next day, the freedman sprinted to the palace, frantically waving the dagger and wailing that Saevinus was plotting treason. It was not long before the entire plot unravelled.

As their alibis fell apart, terrified of torture, Scaevinus and his co-conspirators began ratting one another out, hoping their confessions might just save their lives. Leading the desperate bid for clemency was the knight Antonius Navalis, who, when promised mercy, even went so far as to namedrop Seneca, making him the only one to do so. Amidst the frenzy of allegations, the cowering Lucan supposedly went as far as to implicate his mother in the plot.

Having just returned from Campania to the solace of his country villa, four miles away from the capital, Seneca was blissfully unaware of the tumultuous events. That evening, when the tribune Gavius Silvanus surrounded his house with a cohort of footsoldiers, the philosopher admitted relaying a series of messages between Natalis and Piso, but vehemently denied that they contained anything treasonous.

Impatient, Nero recalled Silvanus and demanded to know whether Seneca was going to kill himself or not. When Silvanus told him that Seneca had no such plans, the emperor brashly handed him a death warrant. As Silvanus made his way back, he was riddled with pangs of paranoia, for good reason. He was one of the plotters. On the way to Seneca's, he stopped to visit his fellow co-conspirator, the Praetorian Prefect Faenius, and asked whether he should obey Nero's request. Heaving a sigh of regret, Faenius told him he had no choice but to.

When Silvanus returned to Seneca, he sent in one of his centurions, who callously refused to let Seneca access his will, lest he make it less favourable to Nero. Unwilling to disgrace himself with a coward's death, Seneca turned to his friends in attendance and declared that since he was unable to show the gratitude they deserved, he would leave them with his most prized possession: the "image of his life". He lamented, "Where were the maxims of your philosophy? Where, that reasoned attitude towards impending evils which they had studied through so many years? For to whom had Nero's cruelty been unknown? Nor was anything left him, after the killing of his mother and his brother, but to add the murder of his guardian and preceptor."

With that, Seneca gave his wife Paulina one last deep and longing embrace, and the two slashed their wrists together. Nero's men rushed over to Paulina's rescue; the emperor's grudge was with Seneca, not her. The great philosopher, meanwhile, suffered an agonisingly slow death. When poison failed to hasten his demise, he slipped into a scalding bath and let the vapours take their course, strangling the last whispers of life from one of the most passionately brilliant and unrelentingly noble minds Rome would ever produce.

Meanwhile, anxious to procure some more tangible evidence, Tigellinus had poor Epicharis thrown in the rack and subjected to brutal torture. Yet, even after days of being lashed, burned, bludgeoned, stabbed, and cut, unlike her upper-class male co-conspirators, she refused to break. With her limbs all dislocated and unusable, when the guards weren't looking, the defiant freedwoman fashioned a noose from her breast band and hung herself in it, disgracing her peers by her honourable conduct.

While his plot unravelled, rather than trying to trigger a last-ditch revolt among the Praetorians and the people, Piso instead slinked off in defeat. As the pieces came together, revealing the full extent of the conspiracy, Nero was horrified. The betrayal had infected even the inner reaches of the Praetorian Guard. In panic mode, the emperor sent his most trusted henchmen to scour the capital for more traitors.

Few were placed in a more precarious situation than Faenius; the treasonous Prefect now charged with investigating his fellow co-conspirators. Although his guilt had not yet been revealed, he could feel the noose tightening around his own neck and could not help but overcompensate. While interrogating Scaevinus, he approached the task with a little too much gusto. Infuriated, Scaevinus spat back at his co-conspirator that none knew more of the plot than himself. This was not the first time Faenius's name had come up. Before he had time to stutter out a comeback, a group of guards tackled him to the ground, and hoisted him into custody.

The emperor entrusted the pursuit of his enemies to his enforcer, Tigellinus, who hounded them down with rapacious severity; having dozens killed, forced to commit suicide or exiled. The Prefect saw this as a perfect opportunity to purge his enemies from the ranks, knowing that the more he pursued the more gratitude Nero would heap on him. Tigellinus persecuted several of his rivals; innocent men, such as Seneca, on the flimsiest evidence, simply because he wanted them out of the way. He knew Nero only needed the most trivial of reasons to condemn anyone he already bore a grudge with.

Asides from those killed, scores of Praetorians were dismissed, and two who earned a pardon for informing later committed suicide. In a great show of gratitude to those Praetorians who had stayed true, Nero paid out an enormous donative of 2,000 sesterces and a free corn allowance. However, even then, he was careful to only send new recruits to deliver the death warrant to Piso, who, like Lucan, killed himself.

Another of Tigellinus' victims was Petronius, one of Nero's confidantes, who had penned the satirical masterpiece, Satyricon, mocking the vulgarity of contemporary Roman society. He had served not only as consul, but 'director of elegance', and was one of the emperor's party animal friends who, in the words of Seneca, "turned night into day". His handsome reputation was perhaps what provoked the envious Tigellinus to accuse him of being involved in the plot against Nero's life.

Taking the initiative, Petronius sent Nero a letter, documenting his orgies and most depraved activities, along with a list of his sexual partners, before slashing his wrists. Unwilling than dying with a whimper, he then bandaged up his wounds, and enjoyed his last day hosting a luxurious banquet, joking with friends and listening to music. He then smashed his ludicrously expensive, 300,000-sesterces wine dipper, made from fluorspar, so that Nero couldn't inherit it, before slipping into one last sleep.

Nero was beside himself; why would anyone want him dead? When he put the question to the convicted centurion Sulpicius Asper, he told was told, "There was no other way to cure your many vices." Before his death, the tribune Flavus, meanwhile, was more direct: "I began to hate you after you murdered your mother and your wife, and became a charioteer, an actor and an arsonist."

As Tigellinus's tyrannical persecution wound down, Nero attempted to maintain his charade of clemency, pardoning some members of the plot, merely banishing others, and refusing a temple be erected to himself, an unprecedented gesture. For their swift work in cracking down on the coup, Nero erected busts of the Tigellinus and the praetor designate, Cocceuius Nerva, in the palace, as well as triumphal statues on the Palatine; an honour even great Burrus had never enjoyed.

The fact that most of the supposed plotters hailed from the senatorial or equestrian classes seeded a deep resentment in the emperor, who began to cultivate an even greater disdain for the nobility. However, as the dust settled, with his enemies all uprooted from their hiding places, Nero felt more assured than ever. The vipers had been gathered together and burned in one fell swoop. Finally, he could look forward to the upcoming Neronian Games with eager anticipation.

Amidst the excitement, a Carthaginian knight called Caesillius Bassus, bribed his way into an audience with the emperor and told him that Queen Dido had come to him in a dream, with some wonderful news. According to Bassus, Dido informed him that back in the day, after fleeing Tyre to found Carthage, she had buried a vast hoard of gold in a great cave that lay, conveniently, beneath his own estates. Although, a decade prior, Nero had denounced Claudius for treating the dreams of others as evidence, having exhausted all other sources of income, the story came as music to his ears. Rather than dismiss the allegation, as he should, he instead took it as divine approval. This, he reminded himself, was the Golden Age; how fitting that the gods would kick it off with so generous a gift.

Too excited to probe any further, Nero immediately sent an army of treasure seekers aboard a mighty fleet to

Carthage. Without even waiting for the prospectors to send word back, he went on a lavish spending spree, expecting to simply refill his empty coffers with the incoming mountains of bullion. With the second Neronian games set to be held in just a few months, orators frothed at the mouth with delight, "Not only were there the usual harvests, and the gold of the mine with its alloy, but the earth now teemed with a new abundance, and wealth was thrust on them by the bounty of the gods".

Frantically dragging Nero's treasure hunters to and fro like an army of headless chickens, Bassus tore up his land, plot by plot. Repeatedly turning up empty handed, trailed by soldiers and excited volunteers, he travelled further afield, certain that the treasure had to be there somewhere. Even as the hunters grew increasingly frustrated, with wide eyes and trembling demeanour, he insisted that his dreams had never failed him before. However, as the weeks turned to months, it soon became clear that Bassus, and Nero, had been foolish to trust what had, in the end, only been a dream. Having stretched the treasury beyond its limits, Nero was horrified to learn that the colossal timewaster Bassus had killed himself.

Although the debacle left Rome in even more dire financial straits, Nero refused to let it rain on his parade. There were more important works at hand. The Second Neronian Games had finally arrived, and the emperor had something special planned; this would be his great public debut. Were Seneca still around, he might have suggested that Nero reconsider; the thought of Nero gleefully performing The Sack of Troy as Rome burned was still etched into peoples' minds. But as far as Nero was concerned, all of his enemies were dead. Who now would dare oppose his artistic endeavours?

With that, Nero kickstarted the festival by taking to the stage and reciting his epic Trojan War poem, Troica, to thunderous applause. The Senate knew where this was heading. Desperate to avoid the disgrace of having the princeps croon on the stage like common riffraff, they flatly offered him the crowns for singing and oratory, declaring no other competitor worthy of consideration. That, however, would not do. Not this time; Nero was determined to win fair and square. Even if the judges were compelled to award him the crowns, he must at least compete. Having thoroughly rebuked the offer, as he left the stage, the adoring audience harangued him, howling and pleading for him to display his other talents, and grace them with his "divine voice". Feigning humility, he blushed and waved, chuckling that anyone who wanted to hear his voice was more than welcome to visit him in his gardens. Instead, he recited another poem.

However, the Augustiani weren't having it. Now 5,000 members strong, their elaborate rhythmic clapping crackled across the theatre like thunder. Tigellinus too riled up the Praetorian Guard, in turn whipping the entire audience into a frenzy. Everyone had heard of the emperor's magnificent musical abilities, and they wanted to hear for themselves. They howled and roared, stomping and clapping, demanding Nero "make public his talents". Like Augustus, Nero continued the façade of the reluctant emperor, modestly leaving the theatre, as the people boiled over into hysteria.

Fearing a full-blown riot, the presiding official Vitellius ran after the emperor, begging him to return to the stage and treat everyone to a musical performance. Nero paused for a moment, soaking in the rapturous outpouring of adoration, keeping the crowd waiting, before suddenly bursting back into the theatre, striding back towards the stage, full of swagger. There, timed to perfection, he ordered his name be thrown into the urn alongside the other competing citharodes. The room erupted.

As the day went on, one by one the citharodes competed anxiously, perhaps even sabotaging their own performances to avoid evoking the emperor's wrath. When Nero himself was finally summoned to the stage, he was preceded by the Praetorian Prefects, who hauled his lyre, urging the soldiers to applaud. The emperor strutted behind, heart racing, barely able to contain his excitement. Behind him trailed the tribunes of the Guard, and his closest friends. This was it. He had waited a decade for this moment. It was, in many ways, his true coming out ceremony.

The room was electric, and the ex-consul Cluvius had to strain his throat yelling over the applause as he announced the emperor would be performing a song called Niobe. Eager to maintain the charade that he had not been expected to be called up to compete, Nero was careful not to dress up in the typical citharode's attire. However, from his posture it was plain for all to see that he was indeed an artist. Once he began playing, he fell into a trance, and simply could not stop. The emperor strummed and strummed, and sang and sang, over and over, until late in the day, delighting the masses, and disgusting the senators in equal measure. All the while, he adhered to the strict customs and rules of performance, never sitting down when tired, nor wiping the profuse sweat from his brow with anything but his sleeve, refusing to be seen spitting or clearing his nose.

As the day came to an end, hoarse, sweaty and all out of encores, the emperor puffed and panted, exclaiming that the award ceremony would be postponed for a day, so he could have another opportunity to sing. He returned the next day to perform once again, exploding with boundless creativity, passion, and showmanship, which he had for so long suppressed. When it came time for the judges to read their verdicts, like an earnest competitor, he kneeled in humility, saluting the assembly with his hands. Of course, the result was a forgone conclusion, but that hardly mitigated anyone's delight. When the emperor arose victorious, the audience rose to their feet in elation and awe, and the Augustiani made elaborate music of their claps. Nero had won what he had always craved; adoration on his own terms. It was an artistic triumph, a triumph of the purest kind.

Chapter 12: Reign of Terror

After his triumphant performance at the Second Neronia, Nero was ecstatic. Gripped by manic delusions of grandeur, he was beginning to buy into his own hype. But, in the summer of 65, just as he was actually starting to feel like a living god, he was ripped back down to earth by a catastrophic reminder of his mortality. His precious wife, Poppaea, for whose love he had killed his own mother, died suddenly; their unborn child perishing alongside her.

It was a bitter shock for the young ruler, one that sent him spiralling into heartbreak and despair. His grief was not only magnified by the death of his unborn child, but yet more vicious gossip. This time, the rumours claimed that Nero trampled his wife to death in a fit of rage, after she chastised him for spending too much time at the races. Although she most likely died from pregnancy complications, the stories spoke to Nero's growing reputation among certain parts of society as an impulsive, violent and frivolous brute.

For his darling Poppaea, ever the showman, the emperor held a public funeral of extraordinary opulence. Instead of simply being cremated in the traditional fashion, Poppaea's body was embalmed with spices, in the Egyptian manner. Nero spent a fortune on oriental incense and perfumes, which trailed her journey to her final resting place, the Mausoleum of Augustus. Fighting through the tears, the emperor personally delivered a eulogy at the

Rostra in the Forum, celebrating her beauty, and her delivery of a divine child. She too was now deified, the Goddess Poppaea, immortalised through coins and inscriptions. Unable to let go of her memory, the emperor found a lady said to be a doppelganger of Poppaea and made her his concubine.

Overwhelmed with grief, he retreated to Naples, where he became increasingly volatile. Whether lashing out in despair, or desperate to refill the imperial coffers, he tasked Tigellinus with pursuing a second wave of political purges. From seclusion in Naples, the emperor wrote a steady stream of letters to the Senate, ordering a spate of prosecutions for various charges of treason.

Having earlier banned Cassius Longinus, a famous jurist and descendent of one of Caesar's assassins, from attending Poppaea's funeral, Nero now accused him of plotting to overthrow and replace him with his nephew, Lucius Silanus. Descended from Augustus himself, Lucius' Silani family had always been in the crosshairs. When Nero first came to power, Agrippina poisoned Lucius' uncle, and then his father, whose deaths were described as "the first under the new principate". A year before the Pisonian conspiracy, another uncle, Decimus, was forced to commit suicide for supposed treason.

Now, Lucius too was accused of harbouring imperial ambitions, and was banished by the Senate, alongside his uncle. However, this was not quite enough to console Nero, who sent a burly centurion to the town of Barium to demand Lucius commit suicide. Refusing, Lucius raised his fists in defiance and dared the warrior and his men to make him. He was swiftly overrun and hacked to death.

Then there was Antistia Pollitta, who three years earlier had witnessed the assassination of her husband Rubellius Plautus; the great-grandson of Tiberius, who Tigellinus had convinced Nero was plotting against him. Despite pleading her innocence to Nero personally in Naples, Pollitta was condemned to suicide, alongside her mother and new husband. Despite Nero's increasing disdain for the Senate and its authority, the senators wilfully turned on one another, signing each other's death warrants without a peep of resistance, lest they make a public enemy of themselves.

As far as Nero was concerned, he didn't care about where accusations came from, or how grounded they were in fact. The more the merrier, especially when the condemned were bullied into naming Tigellinus part-heir, in order to preserve at least a fraction of their estates for their families. Word spread like wildfire of the generous fees, and gratitude, the emperor was handing out to informers for their supposed loyalty. Sensing an opportunity, Antistius Sosianus, the man who at the centre of Nero's first controversial treason trial, wrote to the emperor, telling him that if he were recalled from exile, he would relay some life-saving information about plots against his life.

The emperor immediately dispatched a fleet to swiftly haul him back to Rome. Once home, Antistius accused the wealthy Anteius Rufus of consulting one of Agrippina's favoured astrologers about Nero's impending death. He even treacherously claimed that Ostorius Scapula, the party host who had spoken in his defence during his trial, sought to steal the empire for himself. Fearing the popularity of Ostorius, a war hero from Claudius's invasion of Britain, Nero sent a centurion to murder him at his house in Liguria. When the soldier arrived, Ostorius instead committed suicide, refusing to die by another's hand. Anteius, too, was later forced to commit suicide.

The Senate was not alone in incurring the emperor's wrath. Asides from Lucan's father, Annaeus Mela, a knight of senatorial rank and several equestrians fell too. Poppaea's first husband, Rufrius Crispinus, who had been banished to Sardinia, killed himself when he heard of his impending death warrant. Nero's brutal retribution culminated with the deaths of his old rivals, Barea Soranus and Thrasea Paetus. While Barea was charged with plotting a coup, his daughter, whose husband was exiled, was accused of dabbling in black magic. Thrasea, meanwhile, could hardly have expected to escape unscathed, given his hostile treatment of the emperor, and the popularity his antics enjoyed among the Senate. Asides from being an accursed Stoic like Seneca, he didn't even attend Poppaea's funeral and abstained from her deification.

To Nero, the Pisonian Conspriacy had rung alarm bells about the danger posed by the old Republican nobility. As he continued to persecute supposed threats, he increasingly undermined his original vows, until there was very little façade left to strip back. Having reduced the cowering Senate to a den of puppets, he totally dropped the pretence of their importance and independence. In private, he even began to speak of abolishing the entire Senatorial order entirely, and letting his knights and freedmen run the provinces. In response, one prominent informer felt bold enough to mock the emperor, questioning why he was targeting the senators one-by-one, when he could, with just a word, wipe the entire body out in one fell swoop.

Between the closing walls of paranoia, grief, delusion and triumph, Nero struggled to catch his breath. However, in the spring of 66, with the capital in chaos, victories abroad once again gave him cause for celebration. After years of back and forth, the Persian King of Armenia, Tiridates, finally met with Corbulo to make peace; even laying his diadem before an image of Nero and vowing to only receive it again by the Roman emperor's hand. It was a diplomatic masterstroke, one that would allow a Parthian prince to be installed King of Armenia, but by the authority of Nero.

After a long, drawn-out campaign, Corbulo finally began his return to Rome; a city that, in his absence, had condemned his father and exiled his nephew. As Tiridates made his own way to the capital, he was treated fabulously, given a daily allowance of 800,000 sesterces to finance his 3,000 Parthian horsemen and Roman entourage. He met with Nero in Neapolis, where, despite refusing to lay down his blade, he knelt with his arms crossed, addressing Nero as his 'master'. Nero ironically treated him with more respect than Corbulo, and Tiridates recognised this, remarking, "Master, you have in Corbulo a good slave".

The two travelled from Campania to Rome together in May, and their arrival was to be Nero's greatest spectacle yet. As they approached the capital, which was lit up with garlands and lights, citizens poured out to receive them. Over the past few years, the people had heard so much conflicting news out of Armenia, they were thrilled at what seemed like an overdue victory, or at least an acceptable resolution.

Nero arrived at dawn, and made his way towards the Forum, where a great mass of revellers held out laurel branches, as a symbol of triumph. The crowd was so huge, it spilled out over the neighbouring rooftops, consuming the city. Trailed by the Senate and Praetorian Guard, the emperor climbed the Rostra, the speaker's platform on the western side of the Forum, and sat down in the magistrate's chair, engulfed in a mosaic of military standards.

Tiridates and his entourage followed closely behind, making their way through a lane formed by soldiers, and stopped at the Rostra, where the crowd roared such a deafening cheer, the Parthian prince was visibly shaken. There, he addressed Nero as a god, in whose hands his own fate rested. Nero responded with due grace, thanking Tiridates and awarding him the kingship of Armenia. The Parthian then walked up a specially built ramp, and sat at the feet of Nero, who raised him with his right hand, kissed him, took off his tiara and then placed a diadem atop his head.

The duo then walked to the Theatre of Pompey, to repeat the ritual for a second audience. The Theatre had been gilded for the occasion, signifying it was the Golden Day, and a purple awning was draped over the building, depicting Nero racing a chariot amongst golden stars. When guests looked up, instead of the sun, they were dazzled by an image of Nero, protecting them as he raced across the heavens.

After the re-run, the emperor carried a laurel branch to the Capitol and swung closed the doors of the Temple of Janus, indicating that Rome was finally at peace once more. After a celebratory feast, the excitement got the better of Nero, who indulged himself in a chariot race, dressed as a member of the Green faction. Transcending mere spectacle, over the course of the day, he merged art with life, infusing his diplomatic victory with his cult of personality.

Racing around the Circus was not merely an exercise in hubris. The Circus Maximus was consecrated to the Sun, whose temple was set in the middle of the track. At its core, it was a microcosm of the world itself. The arena was the earth, the channel of its euripus the sea, and the obelisk in the middle, the sun. The 24 races symbolised 24 hours, and the seven laps the seven days of the week. The 12 gates of the carceres mirrored the 12 months and signs of the zodiac, and the four factions the four seasons.

Dressed in the colour of spring, as Nero throttled around the Circus, he followed the path of the sun, with the entire solar system in his orbit. The Circus, which was once supposed to be the site of Nero's assassination, was instead the source of his rebirth as Apollo, the god of light and song.

As he slowly mended his broken heart with adoration, Nero felt it was time to move on. He remarried once again, this time to Statilia Messalina, a lady of abundant wealth, beauty and charm. More than capable of holding her own, Nero's new bride was a keen study of oration, and the art of declamation. Nero was once close friends with her ex-husband, Vestinus Atticus, but had turned on a fickle whim, when his pal made one cheeky joke too many at his expense. Riding a wave of political persecutions, Nero levelled a groundless accusation against Atticus, accusing him of being involved in the Pisonian conspiracy, despite the fact that no one had even named him.

Signifying just how far Nero had strayed from his original vows, his commitments to clemency and due process, he did not even entertain the idea of allowing Atticus, a sitting consul, a fair trial. Instead, he sent the tribune Gerallanus with band of thugs to seize his "fortress" of a house, towering over the Forum, and "crush his train" of young slaves.

Atticus was entertaining guests when the soldiers burst into his home. Enough prominent men had already been purged that he immediately recognised what was happening. Fighting through the shock, and promptly slashed open his wrists, before slipping silently into a warm bath. Throughout the entire ordeal, he never uttered a word. His panicked dinner guests spent the evening surrounded by guards, quivering in fear, before being released late in the night; an image Nero was said to have found hilarious.

After a gruelling year, and an even more turbulent

decade in power, Nero had grown weary of politics. With his closest rivals all dead, it was time for the emperor to take a well-earned break. Finally, he could take that great trip eastwards, to the Hellenic capital of culture, Greece. How better to indulge his primal obsessions with athletics, theatre, and music than with a tour of the great Greek festivals?

One auspicious evening, Nero wined and dined a group of Greek envoys, who expressed their gratitude by presenting the emperor with an array of crowns from the ancient festivals and begged him to sing for them. After singing for his supper, as the Greeks' hearty applause died down, Nero beamed, "The Greeks alone know how to appreciate me and my art!"

The ancient Greek festivals were legendary. Inaugurated in 776 BCE in honour of Zeus, the Olympics began with a series of foot race and wrestling contests, gradually expanding to include all manner of competitions, including horse races, chariot races, discus and javelin throwing, athletics and more. Celebrated every four years, the 211th Olympics were planned for the summer of 65. But for Nero, that was too soon. At his request, upcoming edition was delayed for the first time in more than 800 years, and, in another first, would include artistic competitions; including, of course, singing and acting. Being the emperor had its perks, after all.

While Nero prepared to leave for Greece, his ambitions continued to spiral. Not content to just take part in the Olympics, he would compete in all six of the great Greek competitions: the Actian Games at Nicopolis, the

Olympian Games at Olympia, the Nemean and Heraean Games at Argos, the Isthmian Games at Corinth, and the Pythian Games at Delphi. With a smug grin, he vowed to sweep up all the major trophies across all six competitions to become periodonikes: the victor of the festival circuit. Asides from the Isthmian and Pythian games, which were already due to run while he was there, Nero had all the others delayed, and in some cases, repeated, in order to accommodate his lofty scheme.

Shortly before his departure, another coup was unearthed in Beneventum, but was put down so quickly that little was spoken of it, other than the fact that it seemed to involve Corbulo's son-in-law, Annius Vinicianus. The priestly college of the Arval Brothers offered their thanks for the "detections" of the "wicked" scheme. Despite the alarming rise in plots, Nero refused to change his plans. He knew he was loved by the plebs, and once he was in Greece, he could keep a close eye on the Eastern generals.

Rome's nobility was another matter. The emperor had learned the hard way that in his absence, an ambitious upstart may very well attempt a power grab. Although he had no real rival claimants left, a usurper could attempt to legitimise their position through Claudius's surviving biological daughter, Octavia's sister Antonia.

Some speculated that Nero had harboured a bitter hatred ever since Poppaea's death, when Antonia refused to marry him. Others claimed the Pisonian plotters had planned to reinforce their plot by having her marry Piso. Either way, in Nero's mind, she was too much of a liability. He wasn't going to let anything ruin his holiday.

Unwilling to leave any loose ends, he had her killed. In an act of true malice, he even had Poppaea's young son from her first marriage, his own stepson, drowned by the slaves charged with caring for him.

Nero's trip to Greece would be the first time an emperor had left Italy since Claudius's conquest of Britain two decades earlier. Unlike his predecessor, rather than leaving the capital in the hands of a capable senator with military experience, he handed it to his freedman Helius, along with a license to confiscate, banish and execute men from all ranks, at his own discretion.

In a twist of political brilliance, the emperor coerced some of Rome's nobility to come with him, including the new senator Vespasian and the ex-consul, Cluvius Rufus, who was to serve as the emperor's herald. He even dragged along his trusty lapdog Tigellinus, to lead his Praetorian cohort, leaving control of the Roman Guard itself to the other Prefect, Nymphidius Sabinus.

The emperor would also be joined by his new wife, the 5,000 Augustiani, his wardrobe mistress, his music teacher Terpnus and the usual suspects, his freedmen stooges. Although they were technically there to process embassies and sort through the emperor's mail, the freedmen would also serve his most base desires. Finally, as Nero and his band of misfits finally set off for Brundisium, the Arval Brothers waved him off a series of solemn vows, for the safety of his body, and his empire.

Chapter 13: Zeus

The first stop of Nero's grand tour was Nicopolis, the Greek city founded by Augustus in commemoration of his victory over Mark Anthony at Actium. As the first emperor to visit Greece since the great Augustus, despite his obsession with Hellenic culture, Nero curiously didn't seem to be making the most of his cultural excursion. Unlike most tourists, he didn't visit the renowned religious sanctuaries, or even travel to Athens, let alone study with any acclaimed philosophers, rhetors, or other bastions of Greek culture. However, his intimates knew well that it was precisely the emperor's intimate reverence of Greek culture and mythology that prevented him from doing so.

His innermost circle had heard him rant about being haunted by the ghost of his dead mother, and even the dreaded Furies themselves; hounding him, just as they had Orestes. In his desperation, Nero enlisted the help of Persian magi, or wise men, to summon Agrippina and beg for her forgiveness. The emperor daren't travel to Athens, where the Furies had prosecuted Orestes with their scourges and burning torches. He also sheepishly declined the honour of being initiated into the mysteries at Eleusis, a process that began with a herald sending away impious and wicked observers, lest he be exposed.

Nero's merger of art and life, which had played such a huge role in his personality cult of Apollo, soared to new heights during his tour of Greece, especially once he began to display his talents as a tragic actor. Although he had always loved music and chariot racing, it was theatre that allowed Nero to summon his innermost feelings from the depths of his soul, baring them for all to see. It was also a microcosm for his entire universe; for him, all the world was a stage, and he was the lead actor. Throughout his time in Greece, the emperor performed the classics, Canace Giving Birth, Orestes the Matricide, Oedipus Blinded and Hercules Insane. Asides from Orestes, who avenged his murdered father by killing his mother and her lover, Nero was resonated most with the story of Oedipus.

Oedipus the Matricide begins with the oracle at Delphi warning King Laius of Thebes that a son born to him and his wife, Jocasta, would murder him. When Jocasta gives birth, the paranoid Laius has the baby left on Mount Cithaeron to die. However, the child is instead rescued by the king and queen of Sicyon and raised as their own. Later, the oracle tells this boy, Oedipus, that his destiny is to kill his father and marry his mother.

Keen to put as much distance between himself and his parents as possible, Oedipus flees the court for Thebes. Along the way, he kills an old man in a roadside argument, who unbeknownst to the protagonist, happens to be his biological father, King Laius. At Thebes, after solving a riddle to liberate the city from the dreaded Sphinx, Oedipus is rewarded by being married to the widowed Queen Jocasta, who bears him four children. However, when a plague hits, he once again visits Delphi and is told that to save his people, he must banish the murderer of King Laius. This eventually leads him and Jocasta to realise they are not just lovers, but mother and son. Horrified, she commits suicide, and he blinds himself using her brooch, before being driven from the city by his uncle, to wander the world, guided by his faithful daughter Antigone.

Nero performed the role of Oedipus immediately after the character had been made aware that he had murdered his father and slept with his mother. The core theme of the play was the idea of Oedipus supplanting his father through unintended incest. In Nero's interpretation, the incestuous bond between mother and son represented a journey, where a character conquered a homeland which they had been unjustly denied.

Every noble who had ever consulted a dreambook knew that mothers symbolised their country; so, if they dreamed of having sex with their mothers, it was taken as a sign they would either conquer their homeland or be buried beneath it. Caesar himself, the night before crossing the Rubicon, was said to have dreamed of laying with his mother.

Like Orestes, the crimes of Oedipus were of a legitimate heir breaking a private taboo in order to reclaim their rightful public power. The only difference was that Oedipus was unaware of his folly. In any case, Nero clearly saw both characters as a reflection of himself, and asides from sharing in their grief, perhaps sought solace in their symbolic innocence. Still haunted by the ghost of his mother, his performances were served as force of catharsis, or exorcism of guilt. Pacing the room late at night, he reminded himself that he did what he had done for the sake of reclaiming and protecting what was rightfully his, the empire, on behalf of every citizen dependant on its safety.

Another slightly unusual play the emperor performed was Canace Giving Birth; centred around Canace, the daughter of Aeolus, king of the winds, who lived in isolation on the Aeolian Islands. In the play, a stir-crazy Canace has sex with her own brother, Macareus, who has their incestuous love child cast out to the animals. Humiliated, their father sends Canace a sword to kill herself with. Macareus tries to intervene, but upon realising he is too late, also commits suicide.

Nero performed this obscure myth by taking on the role of Canace giving birth to a child, and tragically following her infant to the grave. Adding a touch of Freudian introspection, he performed the play wearing a mask of his beloved Poppaea Sabina, who seemed to have died of a miscarriage. While some found it touching, cheeky jokes began to circulate among the soldiers present for the tour: "Did you hear about the one about the soldier? Well, a soldier asks another, 'What is the emperor doing?', and the other replies, 'He's in labour!'"

Hercules Gone Mad, meanwhile, centres around Hercules, who is driven mad by the goddess Hera and kills his sons and wife. After consulting the oracle at Delphi, Hercules joins King Eurystheus, and goes on to perform the Twelve Labours. Nero depicted Hercules at the awful moment where, bound to a column, he regains sanity. The hero looks upon the bodies of his family, riddled with arrows, and then glancing at his bow, realises it is he who has killed them.

Once again, Nero's public performance seemed to communicate a desire for absolution; Hercules was struck with divine madness. Therefore, like Oedipus, he was ignorant and innocent of his sins. The symbolism would not have been lost on a contemporary Hellenic audience, well-attuned to the nuances of their mythology. Some may have even likened the emperor to the 6th century BC tyrant of Corinth, Periander, immortalised as one of the Seven Sages.

Periander was said to have been tricked into laying with his mother in a darkened room. When he realised who she was, although the gods stopped him from murdering his mother, she killed herself, and he then descended into tyranny. The original Cynic, Diogenes, even accused Periander of killing his wife in a fit of rage by kicking or throwing a stool at her; perhaps those who accused Nero of the same had taken some artistic license of their own. Self-indulgent as he was, Nero must have been a magnificent actor. On one occasion, one of the young guards posted at the theatre entrance was so shocked at the sight of the emperor bound in gold chains, he rushed over to assist him, interrupting the play.

However, it was Olympia that Nero was most excited to visit. There, close to the gymnasium where visitors had set up their tents for centuries, he constructed an enormous pavilion, alongside a world-class *palaestra* wrestling school near the sanctuary of Zeus. He was careful to treat the Olympics with the due reverence of an ordinary competitor. During a performance of Oedipus Blinded, when the sceptre slipped from his hand, he was terrified of being disqualified, until a supporting actor reassured him no one had noticed, amidst the rapturous applause. Entering the hippodrome dressed in his full tragic costume with high boots and a mask, he always shuddered with crippling stage fright. Sometimes these masks depicted his own image, other times that of his character. In women's roles, it was always that of Poppaea.

Asides from acting, Nero was greedy to snap up all the awards for singing and chariot racing. He even participated in herald contests, announcing his own victories with melodramatic pomp. As he awaited the judges' verdicts, although no one else had any doubt of the results, he trembled with anxiety and trepidation, dramatically announcing, "I have done everything that I should, but the outcome is in the hand of Fortune; you, being wise and experienced men, ought to discount anything due to mere chance." Even though, in some cases, he had already bribed everyone, this never dampened the joy when the judges, whips in hand, inevitably proclaimed, "Nero Caesar wins this contest and crowns the Roman people and his world empire!"

Yet at the Olympics, it was the chariot race where Nero excelled the most, with an awe-inspiring display of determination and grit. Most races, where chariots were drawn by a two or four horse team, were difficult and dangerous enough; only the finest of racers could control them around hairpin bends. Unlike Roman races, which featured 7 laps, the Olympic races spanned 12 laps, crowded with numerous chariots. Competitors went in prepared to crash or be thrown from their vehicles to their deaths. The pinnacle of chariot racing was the 10-horse race, a feat so dangerous Nero once mocked the King of Bosporous for even daring to enter one.

However, at the Olympics, not one to be outdone, this is precisely what the emperor did. And while he probably could have won the trophy without even competing, this was something Nero had spent his entire life preparing for. On one particularly egregious turn, as his horses throttled out of control, the emperor was hurled from the chariot at great speed, crashing into the ground with tremendous force. For a moment, the entire audience held its breath, wondering if they had just watched their great emperor kill himself.

When Nero dusted himself off, the arena erupted into an almighty roar. Refusing to disappoint, rather than flee for safety, he darted between thundering chariots, risking his life, coughing, and spluttering his way back through thick dust to his chariot. This should have technically forfeited him form the competition, but the emperor pressed on, completing the race, and being awarded the wreath of victory anyway. Though the judges in question were traditionally unpaid, they were generously rewarded for their mercy with a supposed whopping sum of one million sesterces. One of the judges at the Isthmian games, meanwhile, was not only handed a vast sum of money, but Roman citizenship.

Unsurprisingly, Nero won every single contest he entered. Sweeping the crowns and prizes all across Greece, to his elation, he was enthusiastically hailed by the Greeks as 'Periodonikes Pantonikes', the All-Conquering Victor. Most cities sent him the victory crowns for his lyre playing before he even arrived, along with the awards for events he had not even entered. When he took to the stage, the gates were slammed shut and guests were banned from leaving. Audience members swore that they'd seen women giving birth during some of Nero's lengthier musical performances, and desperate people scaling the walls, or pretending to be dead. Those who failed to applaud vigorously enough were beaten by the soldiers until they did, and several knights were alleged to have died in the crush of hysterical ovations.

Even the emperor's closest confidantes would be denied access if they failed to show him due reverence. When the upstart senator Vespasian fell asleep during a particularly long performance, Nero kicked him out of his entourage and refused to speak with him. By this point, failure to listen intently enough, or sacrifice appropriately for the preservation of Nero's heavenly voice, could be serious enough to result in an offender being branded disloyal by the Senate. Nero's artistic excellence was even commemorated on coinage, depicting him as Apollo Citharoedus, with long flowing robes, using his right hand to pluck at the lyre in his left.

Nero was having the time of his life. When he wasn't performing personally, he had front row seats to all his favourite athletic competitions. During wrestling matches, he would sit like a judge on the ground, personally pushing back any wrestlers who strayed too far.

At the end of August, while in Isthmus, Nero

inaugurated the cutting of the Corinthian Canal in person. There, the emperor offered a prayer, hoping that the canal would be a great success for himself and the Roman people, notably omitting the Senate from the traditional formula. Throughout his travels across Greece, he expressed increasing disdain for the Senate, to the point where one of his cronies regularly joked, "I hate you Caesar, for being a senator", which never ceases to amuse the emperor. Curiously, it was the tyrant Periander who had first conceived of a canal cutting across the Isthmus. Periander had once asked his mentor, the dictator Thrasylbulus of Mitelus what the best way to govern was. Thrasybulus responded by taking Periander's messenger for a stroll into the fields, and quietly lopping the heads off the tallest heads of grain.

It was a message that was not lost on Nero. Even amidst all the grandeur and glory, he still had some heads to lop off. After receiving a dubious tipoff from a wannabe informer, Nero summoned the Scribonii brothers, who had for so long and so faithfully, governed the provinces of Germany, claiming he had important matters to discuss. Thinking that the emperor probably just wanted to plan out some upcoming expeditions to Ethiopia and the Caucasus, they left their armies behind and headed to Greece with due haste. As soon as they arrived, Nero ordered them to commit suicide. For his troubles, the informer who stitched them up was sent back to Rome and awarded the consulship.

Although he hadn't taken it seriously enough to stay in Rome, Nero was still hung up on the recent rebellion centred around Corbulo's son-in-law. Corbulo, on the other hand, was far too busy to worry about court intrigue. He had bigger fish to fry. Poppaea's chosen governor of Judaea, Florus, had proved a disaster, repeatedly abusing the local Jewish population. When he egregiously pillaged a huge sum of money from the Great Temple treasury, the Jews broke out in revolt. In the ensuing uprising, Florus was expelled to his capital at Caesarea, and the rebels seized most of Jerusalem's defensive positions, slaughtering the Roman cohort left behind. In response, the Syrian governor besieged Jerusalem with a huge army of 30,000, but was dealt a humiliating defeat, losing thousands of men in the ensuing retreat. Once again, Corbulo stepped in, loaning some of his experienced men to the Syrian governor.

With the Romans still struggling, when Nero invited Corbulo to Greece, he assumed the emperor was once again going to ask for him to swoop in and save the day. Upon his arrival, Corbulo was greeted warmly, and then promptly handed an order for his execution. Instead, he chose to die with honour, stabbing himself, muttering "deserved". Nero would later send the out-of-favour Vespasian, who dozed through one of his performances, take charge of the Jewish War, with an army of 60,000 men.

Nero's hostility was not just reserved for political rivals. Although he treated most of his competitors with respect, he slandered the most talented ones outrageously behind their backs. When they walked past, he stared furiously at them, hurling vile abuse, or in some cases, supposedly even paying them to throw the contest. In a grotesque display of narcissism, he forced the long-retired master citharode, Pammenes, out of retirement and, after defeating him, had his statues mutilated.

His conduct was so obnoxious, he was even rumoured to have had one rival tragic actor murdered at the Isthmian games; his throat caved in with the other actors' writing tablets. The emperor's behaviour set an odious example for those back in the capital, where his freedman Helius had a nobleman and his son killed for refusing to change their family name from Pythicus, or Pythian Victor, a title that Nero had earned for himself at the Pythian Games.

However, the emperor also made some new friends during his time abroad. Most famously, he encountered a young freedman called Sporus, who was the spitting image of his dead wife, Poppaea. Nero became obsessed with the youth, dragging him everywhere he went, dressing him up like Poppaea and even treating him like an empress. He not only started calling him 'Sabina', but had him castrated, and 'married' him, despite already being married to Messalina, and his 'husband', Pythagoras.

The antics of the emperor's bawdy inner circle caused quite a stir, sullying all of Greece with their moral degradations. Their behaviour was so disgraceful, it inspired stories of Nero and Pythagoras inventing an absurd game, where the emperor was wrapped in animal hides and placed in a cage. Once the cage was opened, Nero would supposedly hurl himself towards men and women bound to stakes, attacking their private parts like a wild dog, until Pythagoras put them out of their misery.

True to his vision, Nero competed at all the great Greek games; Olympian, Isthmian, Pythian, Actian, Argive and Nemean. Some were even held twice in his honour. Along the way, he was said to have amassed a whopping 1,808 victory crowns. In Corinth, keen to repay the Greeks for their generosity, the emperor delivered an extraordinary speech in Greek, announcing the liberation of Greece. "It is not out of pity but out of goodwill that I bestow this benefaction upon you, repaying your gods, whose care for me both on land and on sea I have never found to fail, for affording me an opportunity to bestow so great a benefaction; for to cities other rulers too have granted freedom, but Nero alone to an entire province."

The Greeks had long taken to calling Nero the "Greatest of Emperors", and now he repaid them by freeing them of the burdens of Roman governance and taxation. The priest of the imperial cult hailed Nero "the mightiest emperor, philhellene, Nero Zeus, god of freedom".

Nero was having the time of his life. But no matter how much the Greeks adored him, back in Rome, under the hedonistic tyranny of his freedmen and flatterers, dissatisfaction was once again rising to the surface. Terrified of an insurrection, Helius had repeatedly written to Nero, begging him to come home, only to be ignored. With Tigellinus abroad, and unable to bring the Guard to heel, Helius warned that another great conspiracy was beginning to spread its tentacles across all of Rome's institutions unchecked.

In his year-long absence, Nero felt that he could control the situation by simply summoning suspected commanders and having them killed. However, when Helius turned up in person towards the end of 67, with an expression of horror etched across his face, the emperor finally realised it might be time to take the threat seriously. The holiday was over.

Chapter 14: What An Artist

After such a triumphant romp of the Greek games, despite the urgency of the situation, Nero could not simply return to Rome. He was coming home a conquering hero and deserved a triumph befitting his mythical artistic and athletic accomplishments. More importantly, the people deserved to bask in his glory. Taking the scenic route back, he rolled up to his beloved Naples in a chariot towed by white horses, through a breach in the walls, as was customary for "victors in sacred games".

Helius trailed the emperor's scenic journey back with nail-biting trepidation. Despite being utterly overwhelmed in Nero's absence, he did have his finger on the pulse. The plotters were hardly being subtle. In Gaul, Julius Vindex, the Praetorian Governor of Gallia Lugdunensis started sending out secret letters to provincial governors and exiled senators. Most of the recipients, still terrified of Nero's tyrannical suppression of the Pisonian conspiracy, immediately informed the emperor of the seditious plans. One, however, did not.

Servius Sulpicius Galba, a senator in his 70s, had been governor of Hispania Tarraconensis, in Spain, for eight years. Curiously, at same time as Vindex's letter, he received an urgent request from the governor of Aquitania to suppress rioting in Gaul. These were interesting times. Unlike Vindex's other recipients, Galba wasn't rattled. He had no intention of running to Nero just yet; he wanted to see how things played out. Unwilling to take a risk, Nero sent an order to the procurator in Spain to have Galba killed, but the wily Galba intercepted it, buying himself a little more time.

In March, backed by the tribes of Gaul, Vindex ran out of patience, and broke out in open revolt. Boasting of his ability to amass 100,000 men, he laid siege to Lugdunum, and launched an aggressive propaganda campaign, minting his own currency and presenting himself as the saviour of Rome. In Naples, Nero had just finished his lunch when he heard the news. However, he was preoccupied; it was the anniversary of his mother's death. Shockingly, his initial response to the dire situation was to not react at all. Instead of mobilising a rapid response and trying to nip the revolt in the bud before Vindex had the time to draw more men to his cause, the emperor took part in a local athletic competition.

Then, at dinner, he received a threatening letter from Vindex himself, but didn't even bother writing to the Senate about the developments for eight days. Despite his bragging, Vindex was a commander without any legions, and Nero's urban cohort at Lugdunum had already proved its loyalty to the emperor. Besides, he figured that his newly appointed governor of Upper Germany, a loyalist, was sure to put the revolt down without too much trouble.

In the meantime, Vindex continued to send Nero a series of increasingly derogatory letters. Eventually, desperate to goad Nero into a reckless response, he pulled the lowest of blows: first referring to him by his biological family name of Ahenobarbus, and then, even worse, mocking him for being a terrible musician, and a sloppy lyre player. This would not do. Growing red in the face with fury, Nero scoffed. How, he asked, could he be accused of lacking skill in something he had devoted so much of his time and efforts to? Preposterous. Such insolence must be punished.

The fire was lit. Nero penned a ferocious letter to the Senate, demanding it exact vengeance in the name of the emperor and the state, with 10 million sesterces offered for the head of the wretched Vindex. Unfortunately, he lamented, he would not be able to attend to the matter in person, as he had a sore throat. He did, however, continue making his way back to the capital, with a series of dramatic processions through his birthplace, Antium, and his favourite imperial villa in Alba Longo. Finally approaching Rome itself, he passed by a tomb decorated with an image of a Gallic warrior being mowed down and dragged by the hair by a Roman cavalryman; an auspicious omen for his dealings with the Gallic rebel, Vindex.

Nero's return to the capital was as bombastic as expected. Dressed in a Greek cloak, with the Olympic crown perched atop his head, and the Pythian trophy in his hand, he soared into the city atop the triumphal chariot of Augustus. However, instead of entering through the traditional arch, he once again burst through a breach in the walls, like a true Greek champion. This was a triumph unlike any Rome had ever seen.

Nero was preceded not by a long list of conquered cities, but of the vast number of crowns he had won, and his acclaimed songs. Behind him, rather than the legionaries, trailed the 5,000 Augustiani, with thick hair and fancy clothes, hysterically yelling, "Hail, Olympian victor! Hail, Pythian victor! Augustus! Augustus! To Nero Hercules! To Nero Apollo! The only victor of the grand tour, the only one from the beginning of time! Augustus! Augustus! Divine voice: blessed are those who hear you!" Sat obediently beside him was the deflated master citharode, Didorus, who the emperor had defeated.

Since the time of Romulus, the triumphal procession had always ended with a sacrifice to Jupiter on the Capitoline Hill. But that was just the beginning for Nero. From there, he rolled up to the Temple of Palatine Apollo, where he offered a sacrifice, and carefully laid out his hard-earned crowns in the bedrooms of the adjacent palace, alongside statues of himself dressed in citharode's attire. Then, he carried on to the Circus Maximus to place all his racing crowns around the Egyptian obelisk on the central spina; raised by Ramses II twelve centuries earlier in the City of the Sun, Heliopolis, and moved to the circus by Augustus. Dedicating his trophies to the sun god, Nero rounded off the exhaustive ceremony with a victory lap around the course.

Although all of this was very familiar to the Romans, after a year abroad, Nero was noticeably different. The emperor who used to address all his soldiers by name now refused to even address them in person, instead writing letters or speaking through intermediaries, in order to protect his precious voice. Dropping the power-sharing charade, he refused to address the Senate properly, and never went anywhere without his vocal coach by his side, who compulsively interrupted those around the emperor, reminding him to spare his throat and cover his mouth with a handkerchief.

When Nero eventually summoned a meeting of his closest advisors, they heaved a sigh of relief. Finally, he was taking the Gallic threat seriously. Unfortunately, when Nero broke his silence, instead of discussing matters of state, he rambled on with a hearty grin about musical instruments, "I have discovered how to make the water organ produce a larger and more tuneful sound". In the ensuing lecture, rather than military strategy, he went through a painstaking analysis of various new types of water organs, offering to exhibit them all in a theatre, so long as, he joked, Vindex allowed.

Now even Nero's abilities as a bagpipe and reed pipe player were known as far as Bithyna, but his artistic ambitions did not stop there. Back in Rome, he took up the popular art of pantomime, where performers enacted comic and tragic forms through imitative movements, in a sort of one- or two-person ballet, augmented by chorus and orchestra. Pantomimes wore flowing robes like citharodes and masks like tragic actors, albeit though with closed lips, and a pair of low shoes. Nero desperately longed to dance like the acclaimed performer, Paris, but was either so hopeless at it, or threatened by mentor's ability, that he had him killed. It was a poor show of gratitude to the man who had once informed him of an alleged plot against his life. The emperor assured himself that once he had defeated Vindex, he would celebrate his victory by dancing the role of Vergil's Turnus.

Three weeks after hearing about Vindex' uprising, Nero

received even worse news. Galba had not been killed after all. Having intercepted his death warrant, when he received another letter on April 3 from Vindex, offering him the leadership and asking him to become the "saviour of humankind", his hand was forced. After careful deliberation, Galba was convinced by a legate from the Spanish IV legion to accept, and gathered his soldiers in Cartagena, where they proclaimed him the emperor. Refusing the title of Caesar, lest it be seen as presumptuous, he instead accepted that of the Legate of the Senate and Rome.

Levying new recruits from Spain's vast population, and a war chest from his allies, Galba created an entirely new legion known colloquially as Galbiana. He even convinced Nero's old partner-in-mischief, Otho, to join the cause, as well as the quaestor of Baetica, and perhaps the Prefect of Egypt. Like Vindex, he started minting his own coins, depicting him riding out with his spear, alongside Spain and Gaul personified, with the goddess of victory stood between them on the globe, holding a laurel leaf in her hand. While Nero had never really taken Vindex all that seriously, the defection of Galba and his allies terrified him, for it elevated the insurrection into a full-blown Civil War.

The emperor was supposedly so shocked by Galba's declaration of war, he fainted. When he awoke, he tore at his clothing, beat his forehead, and proclaimed himself doomed. His elderly nurse tried to reassure him that previous princes had overcome similar problems in the past, but Nero theatrically wailed that his burdens were greater than any that had ever come before. Having gotten the hysterics out of his system, once more uplifting news began to trickle in, he rapidly composed himself, switching from the role of tragic, forlorn victim to defiant, grinning conqueror in an instant.

Invigorated, the emperor held a series of increasingly pompous feasts, loudly lambasting his foes over dinner, and reciting comedic verses afterwards, ridiculing his enemies, punctuated with grotesquely obscene gestures. Although he now claimed to be too busy to attend his theatrical duties, during an undercover trip to the theatre, he warned an actor not to take advantage of his absence. Once again mirroring the tyrant Periander, who forced the women of Corinth to donate their finest clothes to his dead love, the emperor also made all the women of Rome donate money to finance a new temple for his ex-wife, Sabina Venus.

In this time of war, Nero reasserted his leadership, and disdain for the Senate, by firing the two consuls and appointing himself in their place. Gaul, he argued, could only be conquered by a consul. One night, after a particularly debauched dinner, stumbling drunkenly out of the dining room, he boasted of his ludicrous battle plan. Once he reached Gaul, rather than engaging the enemy in a great battle, he would stroll before the rebel army alone and unarmed, and simply weep before them. Having disarmed them with tears alone, he and subjects would then sing songs of victory together, which he had written just for the occasion. Not willing to waste a second more, he began preparing his military convoy. The emperor made sure to choose wagons large enough to carry his assorted props and water organs, as well as an army of concubines, sporting men's haircuts, and Amazon-style axes and shield.

The emperor also had the Senate declare Galba a public enemy and his goods forfeit, while recalling the Illyrian, German and British from their eastern march to the Caspian Gates. With the treasury still empty, and Nero desperate for more troops, he turned to the public for help. However, they responded with such little enthusiasm, he was forced to create a new legion from the sailors of Misenum, and even went to so far as to start training slaves. This was a sorry state of affairs.

The emperor stationed the bulk of his army in the Po Valley of Northern Italy, but rather than lead it himself, he entrusted it to Petronius Turpilianus, who had successfully stabilised Britain, and helped to uncover the Pisonian conspiracy. With donations not forthcoming, Nero flatly demanded that all citizens contribute some of their money to the cause, and that tenants of private accommodation hand over a year's rent to him, rather than their landlords. In typically absurd fashion, he insisted that these payments be made in "new coin, refined silver and pure gold". While this might be appropriate if Nero intended to hand over the coins as a gift to someone, in such desperate times, this was pure madness. Yet, the show must go on.

With food scarce and prices high, the Romans were amazed to see a ship arriving from the breadbasket of Alexandria, not laden with grain, but sand for Nero's court wrestlers. Matters were only made worse by Clodius

Macer, a legate in Africa, also broke out in revolt, declaring himself the champion of liberty and raising an army of his own. The insurrection, believed to have been orchestrated by Nero's old wardrobe mistress, threatened to cut off Rome's crucial supply of African corn. Amidst the chaos and confusion, rumours swirled around that a paranoid Nero was planning to mass murder scores of governors, senators, exiles, and Gauls.

With public confidence plummeting, placards and graffiti popped up across Rome, mocking the emperor. With control appearing to slip from Nero's fingers like sand, people became increasingly brazen. During one of the emperor's speeches, when he scowled that Vindex would soon meet a grizly fate, the Senate cried "You will do it, emperor!", in a manner that implied the emperor himself might soon meet the same fate. During a rare performance of Oedipus in Exile, Nero fatefully bemoaned, "My father and co-husband drives me cruelly to death".

In May, the legate for Upper Germania, Verginius Rufus, laid siege to Vindex's stronghold of Vesontio. Rather than wait for Galba, Vindex rushed north from Lugdunum to meet the attackers head-on. When he arrived, he supposedly managed to talk Rufus into joining him, but Rufus's enthusiastic troops didn't get the memo, and ended up igniting a ferocious battle anyway. In the ensuing bloodbath, the Gallic army was annihilated, with 20,000 said to have been cut down. Devastated at this resounding defeat, a hopeless Vindex commited suicide.

Ironically, Rufus's men were so overjoyed with their

victory, they proclaimed Rufus himself emperor, putting him in an uncomfortable spot. Wriggling his way out of it, Rufus politely declined, arguing that only the Senate had the authority to appoint an emperor. Despite his humility, when Nero caught wind of the proclamation, he sent another army to pursue Rufus, just in case. Remarkably, even now, the emperor declined to lead the army himself. When Galba heard of Vindex's defeat, for a brief moment, he considered killing himself too. Instead, in one last gasp of defiance, he wrote to Rufus, inviting him to join his rebellion. Although Rufus didn't get back to him, several other governors did, flocking in droves to the banner of insurrection.

Resting on his laurels in the capital, Nero awaited on the edge of his seat as things continued to go from bad to worse. This wasn't how it was supposed to go; he was Nero Apollo, champion of all the Greek games! A god among men. The people loved him. Why had they forsaken him so? As his mind raced back and forth, a messenger arrived with a letter, letting Nero know that his northern Italian troops had defected. Shaking with fury and fear, he ripped the letter up into tiny little pieces, hurled over a table and smashed two of his most prized possessions, a pair of crystal goblets carved with Homeric scenes. Galba had executed the emperor's faithful commander, Turpilianus, and now Nero believed that his entire army had now defected.

Preparing for the worst, he had his mother's prolific poisoner Locusta prepare a fatal tonic, and placed it in a golden casket, within his suburban property, the Servilian

Gardens. At least if it came to that, his death would be quick. Then, he sent his most loyal freedmen to the port of Ostia, to prepare an escape fleet, while he frantically tried to convince the Praetorian tribunes and centurions to join him. They refused. Nero had made Tigellinus omnipotent, but in his year-long absence, the other Prefect Nymphidius had seized control of the Guard, and as far as he was concerned, the emperor's time was up. As Nero begged, bitter tears of desperation stinging his eyes, one of the guards grimaced and barked, "Is it such a wretched thing to die?"

Nero's empire was crumbling. The performer within thought about putting on a black mourning costume, mounting the speaker's platform in the Forum and begging the people for their support, or even just their mercy. But what if they tore him to pieces instead? Pulse racing, he frantically plotted an escape route. Should he throw himself at the mercy of the Parthians? Or perhaps flee to the Hellenic metropolis of Alexandria? Unaware that the Egyptian was also on the brink of revolt, he prepared a speech, "Even if I am driven from empire, this musical talent of mine will support me there." That night, with all of the arrangements in place for a swift retreat, an exhausted Nero consoled himself into an unsteady sleep.

After much tossing and turning, the emperor awoke at midnight of June 11 with a funny feeling in the pit of his stomach. Searching for a friendly face, he looked around his bedchamber, and then corridors outside, but there was no one there. He ran from room to room, growing increasingly flustered, as he learned the entire palace had been deserted; his closest friends, his cronies, his cohorts, all gone. Even his private bodyguards had fled, stealing away with his bedclothes and poison box. Only Sporus, Phaon and two other loyal freedmen remained. Everyone else had forsaken him. Nero Apollo was finished.

Tears streaming down his cheeks, he sent for his favourite gladiator, Spiculus, to strangle him out of his misery, but he couldn't be found either. Nor could any of the emperor's professional assassins. They'd all abandoned him. Wailing, Nero darted outside, and resolved to throw himself into the Tiber, weeping, "So, do I have neither friend nor enemy?" Moved by his master's suffering, Phaon suggested they flee to his neglected suburban villa, tucked between the Via Nomentana and the Via Salaria. Nero decided to try his luck. Barefoot, and dressed in but a humble tunic and faded cloak, he wrapped a handkerchief around his face and mounted a horse, riding off with his four most loyal companions.

It was a treacherous night. The sky and earth both opened up, threatening to swallow the party whole. Rain whipped the emperor's scrunched up face, and mud erupted from the earth below, while lightning crackled across the sky above, punctuated with almighty roars of thunder. The heavens and earth were angry. As Nero rode past the Northern Gate near Via Salaria, around the Praetorian Camp, he heard the soldiers enthusiastically proclaim their support for Galba, asking one another "Is there any news of Nero in the city?" They were looking for him. Out-of-favour and severely ill, Tigellinus had neither the political capital nor energy to fight

Nymphidius, and simply went along with the coup. It was only a matter of time before the Senate followed suit.

Racing like never before, Nero's horse leaped over a corpse in the road, which hurled his face covering to one side. Blissfully unaware of the unfolding intrigue, a passing Praetorian veteran smiled and saluted awkwardly, wondering what on earth the emperor was doing. Nero and his freedmen wrestled their way through thick forests of bramble and reeds, before finally arriving at Phaon's derelict villa. There, they told Nero to go hide in a sandpit, but he declined, hissing that he would not go underground while still breathing.

While his entourage dug an entrance into the villa, Nero skulked over to a nearby pond for a drink of water, grumbling "This is Nero's boiled water", while carefully plucking the twigs from his torn-up cloak. It was a humbling, humanising and pathetic moment for the man, who had so recently returned to Rome in triumph, a god among men. Where were his fawning Augustiani now?

Once the house had been breached, the emperor crawled behind his friends through a narrow tunnel, emerging in a dark and dingy room. As he stepped inside, he instinctively hurled his exhausted body onto a bed in the corner, dressed in a thin mattress and a filthy old coverlet, sending dust hurtling across the room. Starved and parched, he refused the dirty piece of bread he was offered, and begrudgingly sipped on some lukewarm water.

With the emperor as comfortable as could be, it was time to address the elephant in the room. Through gritted teeth, someone politely suggested it might be time for him to avoid dishonour and do what he had really come here to do. In that moment, Nero realised how his own mother had felt as the hand of treachery, and its harbingers of death, clenched shut around her. Accepting his fate, the proud prince ordered his men to go fetch some water to wash his corpse and wood to burn it. As they began digging out a humble grave in the wet mud, he asked them to gather whatever fragments of marble they could to decorate his piteous resting place. Amidst their frantic scurrying, he spiralled into despair, tearfully lamenting, "What an artist dies in me!"

Just then, Phaon received a messenger, who handed him a letter confirming the worst. Nero had been declared a public enemy, and must be punished in accordance with the ancient manner. Like a lost boy, the tremoring prince asked what that meant, and Phaon barely had the heart to tell him. The freedman looked down and paused for a moment, before spitting it out; Nero would be dragged naked through the streets with his head clamped in a wooden fork, before being beaten to death with rods and thrown from the Tarpian rock. In a cold sweat, consumed by sharp terror, the great artist hurriedly grabbed two daggers, and poked the points gently into himself to test them. Terrified, he put them away again, howling that the fated hour could not yet be at hand.

Growing hysterical and faint, he collapsed onto his 'bride' Sporus, tearfully begging one of his lackeys to kill themselves first in solidarity, lamenting his own cowardice, "I am living badly, disgracefully". Shamefully, he cried in Greek, "This does not become Nero, does not become him," before steeling himself, "One should be resolute at such times, come rouse yourself!" If all of his life had been one great performance, this was the tragic climax. The show must end on a high note. Such thoughts were interrupted suddenly, by the heavy patter of hoofs beating against the mud outside. His enemies were here. Hearing his cue, Nero wailed a line from the Iliad, "The thunder is beating against my ears of fast-running horses," before finally, with the help of Epaphroitus, driving a sword through his throat.

One of the burly centurions burst his way through and frantically tried to stop the bleeding with his cloak, but a pale and damp Nero gasped hoarsely, "Too late! This is loyalty!" As the last vestiges of life squeezed out of his body, the emperor's eyes bulged from his head. Those around him could do little but look on in horror. At just 30 years of age, Nero, the Bronze Beard who had shown so much promise, the grandson of Germanicus and last of the Julio-Claudians, was dead. Now only chaos.

Chapter 15: Epilogue

Upon hearing of Nero's death, the nobles heaved a long-held sigh of relief, as did the plebs, clients and freedmen linked to his upper-class victims. They took to the streets wearing the caps of freedom granted to slaves on their manumission and partied into well the night. However, his suicide left the Senate in a precarious situation. Between himself and his mother, they had wiped out the Julio-Claudian bloodline, leaving the empire in unprecedented straits. Since Rome's transformation from Republic to Empire, there had never before been a power vacuum like this. It's possible the Senate never intended for Nero to die; they might well have wanted to at least preserve his bloodline. This was no longer an option. With absolute power up for grabs for whoever was bold enough to seize it, it was imperative they plugged the hole as quickly as possible.

Although he was nearly 70, and had no children of his own, Galba already had the Praetorian Guard's support, so supporting him was a no-brainer. His membership in the Sulpicii Galbae family, prominent in senatorial politics for two centuries, helped to supplement his aura of prestige. With Nero dead, the Senate immediately declared Galba 'Augustus', granting him the family name Caesar. While Galba marched towards the capital, his freedman Icelus went to view Nero's corpse for himself and granted permission to cremate and bury him properly.

Nero needn't have worried so much, his funeral was an extravagant affair; his body draped in gold-laced white cloth before being cremated, accompanied by the ever-loyal Sporus. Afterwards, however, rather than being interned in the tomb of Augustus, Acte placed his ashes in the Domitii tomb of his biological forefathers. His final resting place was a porphyry sarcophagus, set atop a white Carrara marble altar and ringed by a low wall of Thasos white marble, overlooking the Campus Martius below.

However, with Galba not yet in Rome, the most powerful man in the city was the Praetorian kingmaker himself, Nymphidius. Despite having declared for Galba, he was having second thoughts. Despite having no claim of his own whatsoever to the throne, he reckoned he could forge one easily enough. Hitching himself to Nero's chariot, he took Sporus into his protection, and remarkably, like the late emperor, began treating him as his own wife. Launching a frenzied propaganda campaign, he began spreading rumours that he was the bastard love child of Caligula. With no emperor to argue otherwise, Nymphidius ran riot, courting the Senate and bringing the Guard to heel, while violently assaulting the memory of Nero and his cronies.

The emperor's statues were dragged from the Forum and smashed; one was even used to crush his favourite gladiator, Spiculus, to death. One of Nero's prolific informers, meanwhile, was brutally squished beneath a wagon filled with stones. Across the city, all hell broke loose, as innocent and guilty alike were crucified or else butchered and torn to pieces by the mob. Amidst the carnage, the young senator Junius Mauricus worried his colleagues would soon wish for Nero's return. Fortunately, Nymphidius's reign of terror did not last long; he was betrayed by the Praetorians and executed as a traitor.

After finally arriving in Rome, instead of embarking on a charm offensive, the prickly old Galba turned to discipline. In an act of great idiocy, he refused to hand out the customary donative to the people of Rome, the provincial soldiers and, most importantly, the Praetorian Guard. Going further, he forced all of Nero's friends to hand back any gifts he had ever sent them, before massacring his way through his predecessors' allies. He was also quick to have Clodius Macer, the governor of Africa who had declared himself emperor, assassinated.

By January 1, Galba had alienated enough men to inspire a rebellion in Upper Germany, where the two legions refused to renew their oath of allegiance. In the ensuing year, Rome would be governed by four emperors, wrestling power from one another in quick succession, soaking the empire in blood. All along the Rhine, the legions declared for Vitellius, a man who Galba had ironically installed to replace the assassinated governor of Lower Germany. Meanwhile, Otho, who had supported and accompanied Galba back to Rome was so furious the emperor adopted another man as his heir that he orchestrated his own coup. Abandoned, Galba slunk off to commit suicide, while his heir was hounded down and butchered in the street.

While Galba had demonised Nero, his old drinking

buddy Otho revived his legacy, not just restoring his and Poppaea's status, but even having himself renamed Nero Otho in the theatre. Hoping some of that Julio-Claudian legitimacy would rub off on him, he started courting Nero's widow, committed 50 million sesterces to the completion of the Golden House, and restored Nero's freedmen and procurators to their former glory. Alas, Otho was defeated in battle by Vitellius in April and, predictably, killed himself.

Upon his accession, Vitellius also performed funerary sacrifices for Nero. For an emperor who died with such disgrace, his successors were certainly keen to bask in his legacy. During the ritual, the Augustales set victims alight, while a lyre player performed one of Nero's songs; to which Vitellius leaped to his feet in in rabid applause. During Vitellius's reign, when someone suggested Sporus play the titular role in a performance of the Rape of Persephone, the poor youth killed himself.

Soon after, Nero's old friend, Vespasian, who had fallen out of favour for dozing off during one of Nero's performances, defeated Vitellius, establishing the short-lived Flavian dynasty. Vespasian would once again demonise Nero, instead honouring Galba, revoking Greece's liberty, opening the Golden House to the public and the dedicating the Colossus outside to the Sun.

In the ensuing years, Nero's story has been immortalised by historians who were hostile to his legacy. While upper class chroniclers such as Tacitus, Seutonius and Cassius Dio loathed him for his athletic and artistic antics, later Christian writers portrayed him as an Antichrist figure, for his cruel persecution of the Christians. However, what is often lost in his story is how beloved he was by the poor masses. In the midst of the year-long Civil War that followed his death, as Rome grew hungry and weary, backed by astrological predictions, some began to hope that Nero had faked his death, and would one day return from the East, a messianic figure, to deliver the empire from ruin.

People continued to model their private portraits on Nero's likeness for years and kept coins bearing his image in their personal mirror boxes. His fans adorned his tomb with flowers, and erected statues of him clad in magistrates' togas for many years to come, accompanied by edicts, as if written by his own hand.

Just a year after his death, the prophecy already seemed to fulfil itself when a man, either a slave from Pontus or an Italian freedman, who looked exactly like Nero sparked off a sensation in the provinces of Achaia and Asia. With Nero's whirlwind tour of Greece fresh in their minds, many were thrilled at the prospect of the emperor's return. A sensational singer and virtuoso citharode, the man bragged that he was indeed Nero, come to reclaim his empire, and began seducing desperate army deserters to his cause with promises of riches.

Though he hoped to set sail for Syria, bad weather diverted him to the Cycladic island of Cythnus. There, he, and his ragtag legion met a contingent of Roman soldiers returning from Syria to declare loyalty to the Praetorian Guard in Rome. Seizing this moment of chaos, the Pseudo-Nero managed to convince scores of them to instead declare for him, while executing the rest. As the rebels turned to piracy, pillaging merchants and arming slaves, one of the centurions in their midst broke free and spread news of Nero's supposed re-emergence.

Desperate to nip this threat in the bud, Galba's appointed governor of Galatia and Pamphylia, Nonius Calpurnius Asprenas, was handed two triremes from the fleet at Misenum and tasked with quashing the rebellion. Once they arrived at Cythnus, 'Nero' summoned the Roman captains and mournfully appealed to their loyalty as old soldiers, beseeching they help him seize Syria and Egypt. While the captains bided their time, dragging out the conversation, Asprenas snuck a contingent of troops around the ship and boarded it. Caught off guard, the pretender was swiftly killed, and his bloody corpse paraded all the way back to Rome.

A decade later, during the reign of Titus, another false Nero emerged in Asia, once again singing and playing the lyre just like the dead emperor. According to his own account, after escaping his pursuers in 68, he had faked his death and lived in hiding ever since. Knowing the Parthians lamented the loss of the cordial relations they had finally achieved under Nero, he sought refuge with them. After all, the Parthians had liked Nero enough to ask Vespasian to honour his memory. Joined by a handful of Asian followers, the imposter travelled towards the Euphrates, gathering supporters along the way, and eventually crossing the border, into the court of the Persian usurper Artabanus. Artabanus was plotting an attack on Rome and thought having 'Nero' on his side would soften his opposition. However, when he learned the man was a fraud, he had him killed.

Then, around 20 years after Nero's death, as Domitian struggled to hold the empire together, a third man of unknown origin emerged in Parthia, where he was treated as if he were Nero himself. He was so revered by the Parthians, they refused to surrender him to the desperate Romans, even at the risk of war.

Towards the end of the century, Dio Chrysostom wrote that "everybody" still wished that the Nero was still around and would remain "emperor for all time". However, the Sibylline Oracles, a series of Jewish and Christian apocalyptic verses based on the prophecies of the Greek sibyls, painted a very different picture. The fourth oracle, completed shortly after the eruption of Mount Vesuvius, saw the event as retribution for the destruction of the Great Temple in 70.

The oracles' Jewish compiler predicted the return of "the matricidal fugitive" who had fled across the Euphrates to Parthia. After years of bloody civil war, "acting the athlete" and "driving chariots", this figure would deliver retribution on behalf of the East, and the oppressed. The fifth oracle, written a century or so later, refers again to a "godlike man from Italy", who, "playing at theatricals with honey-sweet songs rendered with melodious voice…will destroy many men, and his wretched mother. He will flee from Babylon, a terrible and shameless prince whom all mortals and noble men despise. For he destroyed many men."

The third-century writer Lactantius referred to the

oracles, alleging that Nero's sudden disappearance, coupled with his lack of a notable burial place, continued to fan flames that the "first persecutor", who "crucified Peter and slew Paul", would one day return. Amazingly, the fifth century Augustine of Hippo asserted that many people still believed that the immortal Nero would return, either as a saviour or the Antichrist.

The fact that centuries after his death, Nero could still simultaneously inspire such admiration and hatred speaks volumes about his divisive legacy. Trajan, Rome's acclaimed Optimus Princeps, or 'Best Ruler', was said to have remarked that all of Rome's emperors were surpassed by the first five years of Nero's reign. With even Nero's least damning biography written by a man who loathed him, it is hard for modern historians, at times, to discern the truth.

Most of his biographers slip into the convenient trap of simply regurgitating the most salacious, unsubstantiated rumours of his conduct. They write of how he sexually assaulted Britannicus before killing him, fiddled while Rome burned, had a terrible singing voice, raped a Vestal Virgin and stomped Poppaea to death; facts that are legitimised by the undiscerning accounts of Seutonius and Cassius Dio.

However, the details of his life are colourful and fascinating enough without embellishment. Even without the excess, he was a man without precedent. The last of the Julio-Claudians, and the first Roman to ever hold an artistic triumph; a man who simultaneously ruled over some of Rome's finest years, and some of its worst. The

Seneca experiment alone is worthy of its own book. Although Trajan destroyed the Golden House in 104, its ruins remained preserved beneath rubble until the 1480s, when they were accidentally rediscovered by a young Roman. Italy's greatest artists flocked to the site to explore the visionary 'grotesques', the artwork adorning the grottoes, which went on to become major influence on the Renaissance, inspiring Raphael's works in the Vatican loggia.

So many questions still hang over Nero. How great of an artist was he? When he died, did the Greeks weep for their liberator, and the plebians for their protector? Did the Romans, in the dying days of their empire, still pray for the return of their messianic ruler, the singing charioteer who had dared to defy convention? Or did they fear he would return, spear in hand, to land a killing blow to the very heart of their mighty empire?

Either way, Nero's tumultuous reign occurred at a critical juncture of Roman imperial history; one where legitimacy was increasingly becoming a matter of fluidity. Reflecting on his strengths, his passions, his vices, his determination, and his ambition, it is remarkable to think what could have been. Had a descendent of Germanicus been able to cement his dynasty, perhaps it could have endured, and even deterred many of the military coups to come. Or maybe, given the conduct of his last few years, the trappings of imperial life and intrigue were just too great to resist.

He was certainly not the first 'mad tyrant', nor would he be the last. Unlike the genuinely psychotic Caligula, as cruelly as Nero treated the Christians, it seemed that he did initially have good intentions for his empire. His guilt over his mother's death never left him, and without the anchors of Seneca and Burrus, he simply drifted away into fantasy, until he lost all handle on reality. There are many shades of Nero in the later Commodus; another promising young prince turned showman; loved by the people, loathed by the nobility, and killed before his time, leaving civil war in his wake. But, for all his faults, there was never another quite like Nero.

Printed in Great Britain
by Amazon